MILLER | HULL

ARCHITECTS OF THE PACIFIC NORTHWEST

MILLER | HULL

ARCHITECTS OF THE PACIFIC NORTHWEST

Sheri Olson

Foreword by David Miller and Robert Hull

Princeton Architectural Press

Princeton Architectural Press
37 East 7th Street
New York, NY 10003

For a free catalog of books published by
Princeton Architectural Press, call toll free
1.800.722.6657 or visit www.papress.com

Photos
Frontispiece: Bainbridge Island City Hall
Table of contents: Michaels/Sisson House
Works, p 29: Coaches Boat House,
University of Washington

Editor: Jan Cigliano
Copy editor: Heather Ewing
Designer: Stuart McKee

Special thanks to Nettie Aljian, Ann Alter,
Amanda Atkins, Nicola Bednarek, Jane Garvie,
Clare Jacobson, Mia Ihara, Mark Lamster, Nancy
Eklund Later, Anne Nitschke, Lottchen Shivers,
Jennifer Thompson, and Deb Wood of Princeton
Architectural Press
—Kevin Lippert, publisher
ISBN 1-56898-231-3

Library of Congress Cataloging-in-Publication Data
Olson, Sheri (1961–
        Miller / Hull:architects of the Pacific
Northwest / Sheri Olson ; foreword by David
Miller and Robert Hull
        p. cm.
Includes bibliographical references.
1. Miller/Hull Partnership—Criticism and interpre-
tation. 2. Modern movement (Architecture)—
United States—Northwest, Pacific. 3.
Architecture, Modern—20th century—United
States—Northwest, Pacific. I. Title.

NA737.M49 O45 2001
720'.92'2—dc21

CIP
00-048316

Printed in Hong Kong
05 04 03 02 01 5 4 3 2 1

CONTENTS

WORKS

On a rare sunny day during the spring of 1999 a tour of Seattle architecture led me and Jan Cigliano of Princeton Architectural Press down a winding, wooded road on Mercer Island to the Michaels/Sisson residence designed by Miller/Hull. As Amy Michaels enthusiastically showed us through her house, the idea for this book was born. Thanks to Jan for her early support of this project, friendly encouragement, and keen guidance.

Deep appreciation goes to James Russell, editor at large at *Architectural Record* and Robert Bruegmann, professor of architectural history at the University of Illinois at Chicago, who both read early portions of the manuscript and offered insightful advice.

ACKNOWLEDGMENTS

Sheri Olson

Seattle, Washington
September 2000

Sincere thanks to the Miller/Hull Partnership, especially David Miller, Robert Hull, Norm Strong, Craig Curtis, Susan Kelly, Sian Roberts, Scott Wolf, Molly Cooper, Amy DeDominicis, Robert Hutchison, Vanessa Kaneshiro, Amy Lelyveld, and Claudine Manio.

Miller/Hull's clients graciously opened their homes and enthusiastically shared their stories: Annie and Chris Camarda; Kevin Fetterly; Tim Girvin and Kathleen Roberts; Linda Gorton and Ken Bounds; John and Lori Hansman; Ed Marquand; Amy Michaels and Larry Sisson, Jr.; Cynthia Novotny; and Jan Roddy and Marc Bale.

Heartfelt appreciation to the dedicated and loving women at Leah's Preschool, who cared for my son while I worked on this manuscript: Leah Nelsonmoon, Jennifer Driftmeir, Natalie Lee-Wen, Tien McCain, Ebony Steele, and Mandy Stoker.

Thanks to Owen Klinkon, and finally to Phil Klinkon for his thoughtful comments, endless patience, and unfailing good humor.

FOREWORD

David Miller and Robert Hull

This monograph documents the design work of a group practice. As a studio we (the founding partners) have always worked in collaboration. The process of collaboration has been twofold: interactive investigations into the nature and the potentials of a project, and evaluations and criticisms of the correctness of directions proposed. In the early days of the studio, we found that ideas explored by one partner could be brought into sharper focus, clarified, and expanded through conversations with the other partner (now partners and associates) about both the intent and the potential of those ideas. Collaboration operates among the architects in our firm, and also cuts across disciplines in our work with artists, landscape architects, engineers, and clients.

What are the shared intentions and guiding principals of our studio? Miller/Hull's architecture is a search for the correctness of an idea. We are interested in discovering the specific manifestations of a place. We seek out the peculiarities that make a place or mark a special circumstance.

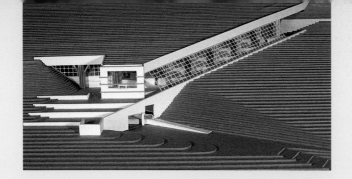

KIMMICK EARTH SHELTER RESIDENCE, MODEL, CLE ELUM,
WASHINGTON, 1982

When we feel we have captured the conditions of the
architectural program and peculiarities of place, we often
look for ways to bend or augment these conditions into
the irregular. These irregularities can often speak of truths.
Our investigations aren't always linear or logical, and
rarely follow the same path, but they do aim for what we
understand as correct. We can't move a project forward
until we feel we have it right. We depend on each other
and the collective wisdom of the studio to be the judge
of this fit.

One can trace the evidence and development of this col-
laborative process by looking at three projects. Two early
projects—one built, one unbuilt—and one recently completed project stand as critical examples of the process
of investigation and design at Miller/Hull.

In the Kimmick Residence, designed in 1981, we were
asked to design a house on a south-oriented hillside in
eastern Washington. At the time we were interested in

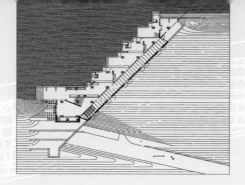

KIMMICK RESIDENCE, PLAN

the emerging technologies of passive solar, super insulation, and earth-sheltered construction. Given the steep slope, we were drawn to the idea of terracing the rooms up the hillside under an earth sheltered roof. In the investigation process, the idea emerged of linking the "terraces" by a linear glazed solar collector canted up the slope and aligned to true solar south. (Interestingly this angle was similar to the path of animals trekking up the steep hillside.) A separation of structure and envelope was achieved by supporting the heavy timber-framed roof from turned wood columns and strut braces and then leaning the window system of glazed garage doors against the roof parapet. Set perpendicular to the slope, the garage doors created a kind of skewed, "irregular," reference to reality. The wood structure was to be purchased from a log home manufacturing company and the glazing system from a local garage door company. This was one of our first projects that looked at utilizing most of the structure and enclosure systems as "off-the-shelf" industrial assemblies.

The Cedar Hills Activities Building, designed in 1979, was our first public commission. We were given a simple program in which to house art instruction and group counseling for a resident alcoholism program run by King County. By looking at the program, we developed an attitude of civil disobedience and refused to inflict a typically institutional kind of building on the occupants. We added porches to the program that functioned as outdoor classrooms. This allowed the building to be stretched to command a greater presence on the site. Due to a very restricted budget, the construction system of the building was explicit: two, parallel structural bearing walls, sheathed in plywood and supported by concrete piers, were braced by large timber V trusses at each end and at the window walls, and spanned by prefabricated trusses. The interior partitions were non-load-bearing, which allowed for flexibility in reconfiguring the space. The porch roofs were clad in corrugated fiberglass, creating a lightness of structure that complemented the solid sidewalls. Throughout the project, we looked to

6

create an appropriate image for this building that would hold some kind of connection with the process of rehabilitation. From our collective intuition, the project evolved into a covered bridge connecting the residents back to their everyday lives. This project was seminal for us as it gave us confidence to take risks with institutional clients, an attitude which has carried forward through the life of the firm.

On the recently completed Point Roberts Border Facility, the process of design was radically different. The challenge was daunting. We needed to create a design that would represent our Country on its national border, fulfill the complex program requirements of two user agencies and meet the expectations of a yet untested "Design Excellence" Program recently initiated by the General Services Administration, U.S. Department of the Interior. In this process, our interest in the rhetoric of the practical was not enough. Form was not the inevitable conclusion of programmatic dictates. Instead the client engaged us in critical and imaginative explorations into the potential of

form. Together we looked for a representative expression of the vitality of contemporary American culture. From this inquiry emerged a building with a soaring canopy anchored by a semi-solid mass. The facility projected both vitality and strength while also suggesting its function as a bridge-like gateway between countries. intense collaboration with the owner helped us to learn to articulate our process. It has helped us substantiate our ideas and validate the risks we take as we have grown, and as we are tackling larger and more complex commissions.

In our minds architecture implies a constant rediscovery of dynamic human qualities translated into form and space. Our approach to these translations is from the modern tradition. We are searching for a rationality derived from clear structural forms and efficient systems of building. At the same time we have tried to invent an aesthetic particular to the firm that is rooted in our region and that exhibits a clarity of intent. We strive to make a significant contribution to a richer modernism.

The Miller/Hull Partnership

As distant corners of the world resemble Seattle more each day—with a Microsoft program on every PC and a cup of Starbucks coffee on every desk— ~~Seattlites conversely fret that the Pacific Northwest~~ looks more and more like the rest of the world. This

MARQUAND RETREAT, NACHES RIVER VALLEY,
WASHINGTON, 1992

The Miller/Hull Partnership takes a different route.
Instead of the well executed but literal pastiche of
the first project or the over-the-top artistic vision of
the second, the firm offers a modernist aesthetic
that is accessible to the larger world. Miller/Hull's
refusal to engage in the either-or, all-or-nothing
debates of the architectural elite is one of the
architects' greatest strengths. They walk a tightrope
to add a civil presence to a landscape that has a
distinct character and native architecture without
being straightjacketed by either. The key lies in
David Miller's and Robert Hull's commitment to
modernism, but it is a regional derivation fueled by

intention of continuing the evolution of modernism has its roots in the designs of Pietro Belluschi and John Yeon in Oregon during the late 1930s and 1940s. Working independently, these two earlier modernists developed a Northwest Contemporary style, characterized by close integration with the landscape, post-and-beam construction, and the use of natural native woods. The economic boom following World War II ushered in a golden age of modern residential design in the region. Seattle architects Paul Thiry, Paul Hayden Kirk, and Victor Steinbrueck were among a first generation of modernists in the region to refine a design language emphasizing revealed structure, natural materials, and glass expanses in houses around Puget Sound.

Miller/Hull has continued this tradition of innovative residential design in forty houses over twenty years—ranging from a concrete-block retreat in the Cascade foothills that recalls Thoreau's Walden Pond cabin to a contemporary version of Charles

and Ray Eames' Case Study house on suburban Mercer Island. While Miller/Hull is known internationally for their houses through publication in *Hauser* and *Ville Giardini,* it is the firm's public work that makes the biggest impact. By redefining a non-existent Northwest urbanism in the astute siting of government, institutional, and community projects, Miller/Hull asserts a new civic presence in amorphous town centers and on the scraggly edges of suburbia. By tethering design to larger urban, social, and environmental concerns—values that trace back to Miller's and Hull's stints in the Peace Corps—rather than surrendering to self-expressionistic urges, Miller/Hull garners a currency with clients that buys them the freedom to stretch the envelope.

FROM BRASÍLIA TO BANGLADESH

If there is one experience that altered both Miller's and Hull's lives and laid the foundation for their future work it was the Peace Corps. Both joined after graduating in 1968 from Washington State

University, where they had met in architecture studio. Assigned to different continents—Miller built houses in a satellite city of Brasília and Hull went to Afghanistan to construct mud brick schools—they sharpened their social consciousness while learning the lessons of building small and efficiently. They both made architectural pilgrimages: Miller toured Oscar Niemeyer and Roberto Burle Marx's recent projects in South America, while Hull visited Louis Kahn's Sher-E-Bangla-Nagar capitol complex under construction in Bangladesh; they both saw modernism under the influence of regionalism.

Northwestern natives, they always planned to return, but when they did in the mid-1970s it was to Vancouver, British Columbia, which was booming, while Seattle's economy was flat. Geographically, the cities are close—only 100 miles apart—but in other ways so far. Vancouver is larger, more cosmopolitan, and, as the "sun coast" of Canada, a destination for

its young innovators. It is significant that Miller and Hull met again in British Columbia, because of the region's role as an incubator of modernism for the rest of the country. Miller worked in Arthur Erikson's office on the Vancouver Courthouse Complex, one of the most influential Canadian projects at the time. (You still have to look north today to see Miller/Hull's contemporaries in the region: Peter Cardew, Patricia and John Patkau, and Peter Busby.) Itching to start their own firm they jumped at the chance to open a branch office for Vancouver-based Rhone & Iredale in Seattle. Backed by the firm's substantial portfolio in public buildings they immediately landed institutional projects. When Rhone & Iredale dissolved in 1977, the two formed the Miller/Hull Partnership.

A thumbnail psychoanalysis of the pair suggests that Miller is the left-brain rational one and Hull the right-brain intuitive one. But it is not always easy to

POINT ROBERTS BORDER STATION, POINT
WASHINGTON, 1997

BAINBRIDGE ISLAND CITY HALL, BAINBRIDGE
ISLAND, WASHINGTON, 2000

waterlogged site, with a small service core that divides it into two open spaces. Within the confines of a tight budget, Miller/Hull creatively manipulated standard residential construction techniques such as exposing prefabricated wood trusses for a low-tech look. At both ends of the building, wood struts angle up from the center of the porches to mirror the V-shape of the truss. This super graphic gives the project a presence belying its modest size.

Miller/Hull's commitment to sustainable design began early. During the early 1980s they designed several earth-sheltered houses, including the Kimmick residence in Cle Elum, Washington. The design surgically cuts across a steep hillside with a diagonal array of rooms displaying a rigor unusual for the genre. They brought their interests in energy and resource conservation to bear for the first time on institutional work with a water-quality testing lab in Seattle in 1986. A three-story mechanical core through the center of the building houses an

energy-efficient heat-exchange system for the laboratories. To take advantage of the Lake Washington Ship Canal location, Miller/Hull urged the Army Corps of Engineers to allow the extension of the building's concrete frame out over the water, facilitating the natural ventilation of the offices.

Farther up the ship canal sits a breakthrough project for Miller/Hull, which brings together the structural expressiveness, low-tech sensibility, and layered transparency that are the hallmarks of their of work. This classroom for Seattle Central Community College's marine-technology program, completed in 1987, sits beneath the Ballard Bridge. Surrounded by dry docks, commercial fishing fleets, and marine manufacturing, it draws on the waterfront's industrial vitality without lapsing into nostalgia for the past. The design is a simple box that appropriates the structure for its articulation. Here the light steel framework acts as a minimal billboard establishing a presence for the school within the waterfront

MARINE TECHNOLOGY FACILITY, SEATTLE CENTRAL
COMMUNITY COLLEGE, SEATTLE, WASHINGTON 1987

community. A large shed roof starts low on the land-side of the building and rises up two stories high toward the water. The palette of inexpensive, low-tech materials changes from solid concrete block and corrugated metal siding on the north to layers of steel pipe columns, steel tie rods, and a horizontal wood sun screen on the south. Glazed garage doors roll up, opening the classrooms to the active waterfront. Solid office modules punctuate the six-bay facade, popping out into the double-height open-air circulation deck. Seattle Central establishes the tension between volume and structural frame, between enclosure and openness, between the vernacular and the modern that energizes the firm's work.

RETREAT INTO NATURE
A series of small cabins on Decatur Island provides an accurate barometer of the firm's development. Many of the ideas that make Miller/Hull's public work expressive—the spare form, structural expres-

siveness, and exaggerated graphic sensibility—are exhibited here at a smaller scale in a natural setting. Decatur, the most isolated of the San Juan Island chain, is only reachable by private passenger-only ferry or by small plane. As planned in the early 1970s, a circle seventy-five or one-hundred feet in diameter circumscribes each residential site in the 485-acre development, with the remaining rolling forested slopes and rocky beaches held in trust. There are no private cars in the development and no stores; so provisions and building materials are shipped in by barge.

The inverted roof of the firm's first design for the island, the 1987 Gorton/Bounds cabin, mirrors a mossy bowl on a hillside overlooking the water. From a flat area over the entry on the east side of the house, the roof slopes up and out in three directions, projecting the main living area toward the panoramic view of the Canadian coastline thirty miles away. The perimeter of the compact 600-

RODDY/BALE HOUSE, BELLEVUE, WASHINGTON, 1987

square-foot cube is a framework of double-height heavy-timber columns and cross bracing with two-story tall windows set five feet inside the structure. The strict geometry of the structure packs a graphic punch, giving the cabin a visual impact that belies its diminutiveness. Gorton/Bounds demonstrates the architects' resourcefulness with tight budgets and off-the-shelf materials to link inside and out. The oversized window walls are glazed wooden garage door panels stood on end with joints sealed and covered by wood battens with hinges at operable end panels. In a narrow core containing the kitchen, bathroom, and sleeping areas, a hori-

directly from the structure, but where the first resembles an engineer's loading diagram, Novotny recalls the raised flaps of forest service fire watchtowers. Perched on a cliff, a short bridge connects the hillside to the main living space on the upper level. Glass wraps all four sides of the single open room, which gives one a strong impression of still being outside. Its gable roof, compact volume, and overdrawn wood trim around the windows lend the cabin the iconic quality of a child's drawing of a house.

A third project built in 1994 on Decatur is the most widely published Miller/Hull project, due perhaps to a charismatic mix of the vernacular and the modern. It is larger than the previous cabins, forcing a change in siting strategy that translates into Miller/Hull's later public work. The weekend getaway comprises two volumes set at a forty-five-degree angle to each other, separating the guest quarters and an office from the main house. In the resultant juncture is an outdoor entry space covered by a glazed roof and faced with a large glazed barn door along the north, which can close for wind protection. In this way, the house opens to the landscape creating a geometry that adds interest to the simple volumes.

The island cabins pose a conflicting desire: to enjoy a private piece of the Pacific Northwest, without paving over the wilderness that is the attraction in the first place. The 1992 Marquand retreat comes closest to resolving this dilemma — due to a client that did not feel the need to equip his vacation house with all the luxuries of modern life. Instead this 450-square-foot primitive hut is off the power grid: Kerosene lanterns provide light, a wood stove heat, and a picnic cooler serves as the weekend refrigerator. A truck hauls water to the remote site in the Cascade foothills and stores it in a tower over a gravity fed shower and toilet. The spare design recalls the economy of means learned in the Peace Corps, but its scale imparts a monumentality befitting the raw beauty of the landscape.

Practical considerations were key in selecting the retreat's industrial materials, since it sits in an area prone to wildfires and intruders. The exterior walls are concrete block, and metal shutters lock down over each opening. A roll-down steel door protects a ten-foot square opening in the center of the south facade. Clerestory windows between the two overlapping planes of the roof allow sunlight to penetrate into the two-room interior. One of the corrugated metal planes floats over the house engaging the tower on the north and then projecting out to cover a porch on the south. A single off-center column holds up a cantilevered-edge beam and frames a view of the surrounding basalt cliffs.

AT HOME IN SUBURBIA

Sylvan retreats are part of the region's mythology, but weekday suburban reality resembles that of any other sprawling metropolitan area. One difference is a stronger tradition of innovative residential design. The enthusiastic embrace of modern architecture by the Pacific Northwest's young middle-income families was so notable that *Architectural Record* devoted the October 1953 issue to modern houses in Washington and Oregon. While staying the post-war course, Miller/Hull's houses translate today's mix of work and family into flexible and forgiving spaces tolerant of the messiness of everyday life.

Residential clients who come to Miller/Hull looking for a "Northwest" design are flexible as to what that means. It is less about materials — glass, steel, and concrete are as palatable as wood — than the way the house embraces the landscape. The Roddy/Bale

ART STUDIOS, EVERGREE[
OLYMPIA, WASHINGTON, [

residence in Bellevue, Washington, built in 1998, exemplifies this trait. The house sits off a country lane, on the shores of a small lake but only ten minutes from Microsoft's Redmond campus. Miller/Hull's design demonstrates a keen understanding of the site's hot points. The house is a slender bar that straddles the long strip of land and divides it into two distinct outdoor rooms. The north side features a tranquil progression from the street through the woods and across a wide lawn to the house; the backyard opens to the lake. A notch carved underneath the upper floor of the house allows a direct connection between the front and back yards. Glass and aluminum industrial garage doors enclose this outdoor room and slide open to shift the design's transparency from the visual into the physical realm. The metal siding, which varies in color from an olive green to a tawny rose depending on the brightness of the sky, underscores this ephemeral quality.

MICHAELS/SISSON RESIDENCE, MERCER ISLAND,
WASHINGTON, 1998

The Michaels/Sisson house, built in 1998 on suburban Mercer Island, floats planes of corrugated metal siding and glass on a structural steel grid A vertical ribbon of glass splices the front facade and penetrates the two-story living space to a glazed garage door that opens onto a deck out into a wooded ravine. Inside, the design is compact yet open with dynamically interlocking interior spaces with large panels that slide to open rooms in varying combinations. Suspended between the children's playroom below and the main living area above is an office built into a widening in the stair. While mining the expressive potential of industrial materials and revealed structure, the design balances the coolness of exposed steel and concrete block with the warmth of the glue-laminated timbers and wood panel floors. Together the two houses form a study in the variations possible within a building type, and with limited budget and material palette.

EXURBIA'S CIVIC FACE

The region's tradition of innovative residential design does not always translate into the public sphere. Government, institutional, or commercial buildings tend to fall into two categories: the pumped-up scale of a Northwest Style house or the bland corporate aesthetic. Avoiding these pitfalls, Miller/Hull creates a civic style tied to the specificities of place while drawing on the modern principles that make their houses unique. In contrast to traditional institutional buildings that rely on symmetry and solidity to convey gravity and longevity, Miller/Hull redefines civic architecture with thin planes, geometric volumes, and floating surfaces.

An exceptional example is the firm's 1995 classroom building for the Olympic College in Shelton, Washington—winner of a 1998 National American Institute of Architects (AIA) Honor Award. Here

OLYMPIC COLLEGE, SHELTON WASHINGTON, 1995

Miller/Hull returns to the animated shed they first used at the Seattle Central Marine Technology Center in 1987. A vast roof hovers over classrooms running along the north and the covered open-air walkway connecting them along the south. Faculty offices puncture the classroom wall, articulating this elevation and providing a more intimate scale. The roof, rising over its 100-foot length, culminates in a dramatic double-height porch held aloft by a steel beam supported on a "V" of slender steel pipes. It is a simple yet innovative detail that appears off balance; it captures the eye and creates an indelible image.

Miller/Hull's emphasis is on the expressive potential of ordinary construction rather than on high-craft but high-cost details. This is in part due to budgets that will not support overly precious detailing, but also to Miller and Hull's Peace Corps days

and the principle of doing more with less. They achieve textural variety and depth through innovative yet straightforward handling of ordinary materials. At Olympic College, fine grained natural wood siding is juxtaposed against manufactured wood panels. Oversized wood battens cover the vertical joints between panels every four feet and have exposed fasteners to contrast roughness with fineness.

The breakthrough for Miller/Hull at Olympic College lies in its saturated colors. Before this building the firm's projects were monochromatic. At Olympic College the firm drew on the varied hues of the Pacific Northwest—the bright puce green of young ferns, the raw red of decomposing cedar logs, the tart yellow of lichen—and applied them with a pop art sensibility in large fields. Olympic College's color palette, jumbo textured siding, and oversized

One drawback to the figure-field approach is that the solids tend to be more prominent in Miller/Hull's work than the voids. The designs are driven by volumes rather than by space. The strongest spatial quality is the relationship between the inside and outside. Like early International Style modernists, Miller/Hull focuses on volumes and the way materials wrap them or on a structural frame enveloped by a protective screen. Often they leave large surface areas unbroken—whether it is metal siding, masonry, or wood—to give a stretched, taut effect, imbuing projects with characteristic lightness and transparency.

HIGH POINTS IN A PROSAIC LANDSCAPE

Miller/Hull considers all building types to be within the purview of the architect. This philosophy brings a new level of thoughtfulness and creativity to the utilitarian structures that are the backdrop of community life. On nearby Vashon Island, a recycling

center represents the firm's commitment to the design of prosaic infrastructure and the willingness of the client, King County, to go beyond a big box—as long as it does not cost more. Miller/Hull accomplished this by subtly manipulating the volumes and materials. Narrow and wide rib corrugations of metal siding juxtapose to create texture and visual interest. The crisply cut windows and vents that puncture the metal skin are framed by knife-edged metal trim. The translucent panels that pop up a few inches above the roof to break the cornice line are one of several simple but sophisticated gestures that distinguish the pragmatic project.

An aluminum filigree of local flora and fauna by artist Deborah Mersky, which encircles the six large portholes to the recycling pit, makes it clear that this is no ordinary dumpsite. This eco-conscious community's unusual mix of farmers, artists, and families socializes as it sorts newspapers, glass, and plastics. Their recycling center on Vashon Island is an unusual symbol of civic pride; it is the result of Miller/Hull's sensitivity in recognizing the activity and creating an architectural place for it to occur.

A water pollution control laboratory on the Willamette River in Portland, Oregon, is another example of a utilitarian project with a public face. At 40,000 square feet, it is a step up in scale for the firm. A working demonstration of storm-water treatment on the park-side site illustrates the building's purpose as a water-quality testing facility. Visitors peek into the laboratories through windows cut in a public corridor that extends the length of the building ending in a bridge out over a filtration pond. The overscaled roof and exposed steel structure — painted grass green in a gesture to the St. John's suspension bridge that soars overhead — create an inviting presence along the waterfront.

Scuppers and downspouts emphasize the fact that roofs are a major source of storm-water runoff in urban areas. The building's riverfront facade has a syncopated rhythm of operable windows within a glass curtain wall protected by a brise-soleil of metal grating. In place of the isolating rabbit warren of most laboratories, scientists perform tests in a loft-style space with daylit communal areas that encourage interactions and create a humane work environment.

NEW DIRECTIONS

At the twenty-year mark in Miller/Hull's practice, two recent projects convey the culmination of earlier investigations while suggesting new directions. At first glance the skeletal steel structure of the Point Roberts Border Station and the volumes and taut skin of the Bainbridge Island City Hall do not appear to have much in common; both of these civic projects, however — one for the federal government,

WATER POLLUTION CONTROL LABORATO
OREGON, 1997

the other municipal—share an underlying physical
and phenomenological transparency that links modernism to an open democratic society.

Point Roberts, Washington, is a geographic fluke.
The four-square-mile appendix of land became
United States territory in 1846 when the Oregon
Treaty drew the border along the 49th parallel, cutting off the southern tip of British Columbia. When
increasing traffic required a larger facility, the U.S.
General Services Administration (GSA) made it the
first border station under a new Design Excellence
Program to achieve top-quality design for federal
building projects. The GSA was not disappointed: the
project won a National AIA Design Award in 2000.

Sightlines drove the design. Border agents must
be able to monitor two outdoor inspection areas from
the porthouse: one for cars passing through the
checkpoint and a pull-off area for further inspection.

PIERCE COUNTY ENVIRONMENTAL SERVICES BUILDING,
UNIVERSITY PLACE, WASHINGTON

Small portions of the porthouse are opaque for holding cells and other secure areas. A narrow bar contains the porthouse and is solid along the east where traffic stacks up waiting to cross at the Canadian border station. Two buoyant steel canopies emerge from the wood-clad carapace of the porthouse and soar up to their highest point over the outside lanes for trucks. A pair of masts strung with steel cable picks up the 100-foot cantilever of the main canopy, recalling sailboats in nearby marinas.

The scheme displays the clarity characteristic of most of Miller/Hull's work, but there is a new dynamism in the way it pushes structural rationalism to an extreme. There is a split between the canopies' steel structure and the wood porthouse, as if the two programs and materials resist joining together. The tension between them is almost palpable. A glass

and steel skylight weaves them together creating a layered, transparent space merging the rational and the experiential. The result is a project at ease on a remote, wooded site while projecting a dignified federal presence.

At 24,000 square feet, the Bainbridge Island City Hall is Miller/Hull's largest civic project to date. The mayor's office, city council chambers, and administrative departments cluster around an internal skylit main street. Citizens grasp the hubbub of everyday bureaucratic functioning from the cafeteria-style service counters down the center of the double-height space. The clipped eaves, metal roof, and wood-batten siding recall the island's barns and timber mills. The design responds to a public yearning for a building that is not ostentatious and yet projects a strong civic presence. Neither new urbanist nor old, the project's astute siting emphasizes

FESTIVAL PAVILION AT SEATTLE CENTER, SEATTLE,
WASHINGTON

connections to the Bainbridge Performing Arts Facility and an outdoor Farmer's Market, creating a new civic center in an amorphous downtown.

As one of ten national AIA Earth Day 2000 projects, the Bainbridge City Hall reflects the firm's commitment to sustainable design. A double-height internal street draws natural light deep into the interior of the project—no desk is farther than twenty feet from daylight—and facilitates natural ventilation through operable windows. The project's wood framing is the region's first major installation of wood from a forest certified for its stringent stewardship practice; finish materials are recycled, nontoxic, or non-ozone depleting. At a time when sustainability tends to extremes—the eco-purists versus the willfully oblivious—Miller/Hull's talent for

On the drawing boards or under construction are designs that confirm Miller/Hull's continuing dedication to integrating aesthetic, structural, and environmental issues: a steel and glass loft building on the edge of Seattle's downtown, a light rail transit station in Tacoma, and a spare interpretive center in the Cascade Mountains. By widening the scope of their undertaking rather than narrowing the focus, the firm bypasses polarizing debates and opens the door to a critical practice. To be critical, according to social and cultural historian Raymond Williams, is to develop an active and complex relationship with a situation and its context. In Miller/Hull's case it means working as modernists within the traditions of a local culture while offering building blocks to the future.

LEFT: THE GORTON/BOUNDS CABIN OVERLOOKS
THE SAN JUAN ISLANDS.

BELOW: SECTION SHOWING SLOPED ROOF OVER
THE MAIN LIVING SPACE

Gorton/Bounds Cabin

Decatur Island, Washington 1987

The significance of this small, 600-square-foot cabin 31 goes beyond the fact that it was the first retreat Miller/Hull designed on Decatur Island, or that it was their first widely published project. Instead its importance lies in capturing the unpredictable, alchemic moment when Miller/Hull's earlier experiments come together to create a design with clarity of structure and of purpose. The clients, a young family of three, facilitated the architects' progress by requesting a retreat that was distinct in form, function, and feel from a conventional house. They also wished to minimize the barriers between their indoor life and an outdoor view that stretches as far as Canada. Within a structural framework of posts-and-beams and cross bracing, Miller/Hull created an inverted roof that merges the interior with the exterior.

A narrow footpath along a mossy slope leads to the cabin's entry centered on the east elevation. From a flat area over the door the roof slopes up and out in three directions over a main living space projecting

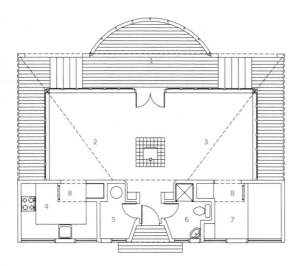

1 **PORCH** 2 **DINING ROOM** 3 **LIVING ROOM**
4 **KITCHEN** 5 **STORAGE** 6 **BATHROOM**
7 **BEDROOM** 8 **LADDER TO LOFT ABOVE**

32

out to the panoramic view. On three sides a double-height wall of windows sits five feet inside the structure to shade the glass and further blur the boundary of the exterior wall. The windows are made of glazed wooden garage doors, standing on end with full height operable panels for ventilation. This subdivided window wall is more transparent and less expensive than large plate glass, since the wood grid breaks up the reflections on glass that can make it opaque.

The ninety-inch-wide core on the uphill side contains a bedroom, kitchen, and bathroom on the first floor, with ship's ladders leading up to two sleeping lofts. Cedar siding wraps around the core from exterior to interior forming a backdrop for the glass-enclosed living room and underscoring the sense of being outside. The solid core is balanced by a horizontal band of ribbon windows that run the width of the entry facade, tying together a series of standard wood-frame windows. The monolithic quality provides a backdrop for the main living space. A spacious semi-circular wooden deck cantilevers out over the steep drop to the rocky beach.

LEFT: GLAZED WOODEN GARAGE DOORS ENCLOSE THE
MAIN LIVING SPACE.

RIGHT: THE DECK CANTILEVERS OVER A STEEP DROP
TO THE WATER BELOW.

BELOW: EXPANDED AXONOMETRIC OF TYPICAL
STRUCTURAL BAY

RIGHT: ROOF SLOPES UP TO A DOUBLE-HEIGHT
PROMENADE.

OVERLEAF: THE SOUTH FAÇADE REFLECTS
SEATTLE'S ACTIVE SHIP CANAL.

Marine Technology Facility
Seattle Central Community College

Seattle, Washington 1987

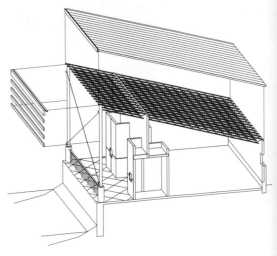

36 The ship canal connecting Seattle's three main bodies of water—Lake Washington, Lake Union, and Puget Sound—is lined with an agglomeration of dry-docks, commercial fishing fleets, and marine manufacturing and traversed by a series of drawbridges. At the foot of the cast-iron Ballard Bridge is Miller/Hull's classroom building for Seattle Central Community College's marine-technology program. Students prepare for maintenance and operational positions aboard tugs, ferries, and fishing boats amidst a working waterfront. The project's exposed structure, metal siding, and shed roof reflect its maritime setting while Miller/Hull layers these elements to achieve a lightness and transparency that characterizes their later work.

The 6,000-square-foot building is the second phase of a master plan the firm developed in 1980 for the two-acre site. In the first phase the muddy lagoon was dredged to bring water up to a concrete bulkhead, which forms a plinth for the new structure. The north side of the building sits on the back property line, creating a security wall that screens the site. From here a corrugated metal shed roof starts low and slopes up toward the south to create a two-story facade on the water. On the short west end of the building the roof turns up in a gesture toward the bridge.

LEFT: LAYERS OF STRUCTURE AND SUNSCREEN
DEFINE THE EDGE OF THE PROMENADE.

BELOW: ELEVATION OF SOUTH FACADE

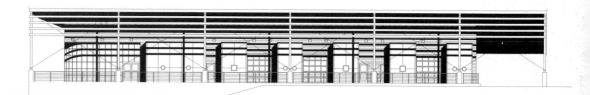

A double-height open-air promenade along the canal simulates the experience of being on a ship's deck while taking advantage of the mild climate to connect three classrooms, a library, and a lunchroom. Standard two-foot-square glazed garage-doors roll up to open the classrooms to the waterfront and alternate with the solid office and storage modules that pop-out into the colonnade. The last of the six structural bays is open on the east end as a gateway into the boatyard. Tube-steel columns sit on a concrete base on top of the concrete plinth, with steel tie rods threaded through a section of pipe that is cut and welded at the top and bottom of each column as lateral stiffeners. The bright-red rods cross at the center of each bay defining the edge of the building. At the top of the arcade, a glue-laminated sunscreen blocks the high summer sun adding a minimalist cornice to the classical composition. During winter, low light penetrates the glass garage-doors to warm the extra gravel underneath the exposed concrete slab for passive solar heating.

The design juxtaposes off-the-shelf materials and structural expressiveness with elegant details evocative of handcrafted boats. Along the colonnade runs light stainless-steel cable railing with a polished teak cap. The metal flashing, which trims the medium-density-fiberboard office modules, resembles the banding on steamer trunks. The refined detailing and elegant proportions of the structure combine with the waterfront's straightforward vocabulary to produce a seamless marriage of the classical and the vernacular.

41

LEFT BELOW: SECTION OF SECOND-FLOOR ADDITION
TO EXISTING ART SCHOOL

RIGHT: GLAZED GARAGE DOORS OPEN THE DRAWING
STUDIO TO THE WOODS.

Art Studios
Evergreen State College

Olympia, Washington 1990

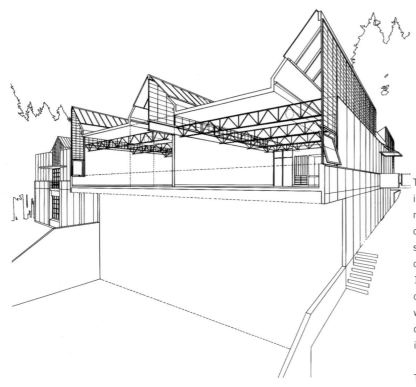

42

The Evergreen State College is known for its radical interdisciplinary program. There are no prescribed majors; instead students create their own curricula, often with an environmental emphasis. Built from scratch during the early 1970s, the campus is a series of neo-brutalist concrete megastructures isolated in 1,000 acres of pristine woods. When the college's art department outgrew the facility, the faculty wanted warehouse space in nearby Olympia, but the regents charged Miller/Hull with expanding the original building on the edge of campus.

To satisfy the faculty's longing for loft space, Miller/Hull's design has an open, industrial feeling inside an angular metal and glass addition on top of the existing one-story concrete building. To seismically upgrade the original building, a graphic "X" of steel bracing is bolted to the exterior of the old structure below. Next door is a new two-story studio that picks up the theme of the first building with a matching concrete base and steel and glass above. Connecting

BELOW: EAST ELEVATION

RIGHT: TRANSLUCENT PANELS OVER CLEAR GLASS
WINDOWS DIFFUSE LIGHT AND OPEN UP VIEWS

OVERLEAF: GLAZED ENTRY CONNECTS SECOND-FLOOR
ADDITION AND NEW TWO-STORY STUDIO.

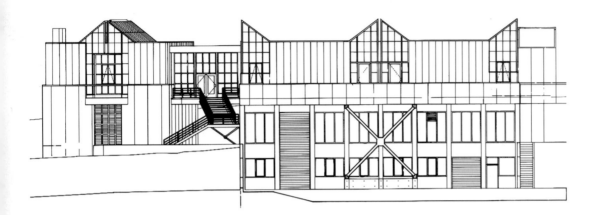

44 the buildings at the second floor is an entry and gathering space that spans a passageway between two exterior courtyards. The first floor of the new structure houses a ceramic studio and the second floor is a single, large figure drawing studio. In the addition above the existing building are three new painting studios and a critique room linked by a gallery.

The design is unusual for Miller/Hull in that it melds inside and outside through a series of skylights instead of through wall openings. In essence the building's section is the lighting concept. Miller/Hull tested the design's viability in a series of year-round daylighting studies on large-scale models at the University of Washington's lighting lab. Students work on easels and use the walls as pin-up space in the painting studios, as natural light enters through large monitors along two parallel edges of the studio. The monitor's vertical face is comprised of translucent fiberglass panels and the sloped portion of clear glass to allow both diffused light and a sense of the sky above. At the corner of each studio the panels step down to an eye-level clear glass window for a view out to the trees. In the new building's drawing studio, students work around a central still life or figure model under a central clear glass skylight. Glazed roll-up garage doors at each end of that space open onto two balconies.

The school's informal warehouse atmosphere is conducive to splashed paint and other creative additions by students. The floor is polished concrete, the interior walls are drywall on steel studs, and the ceiling is exposed steel bar joists threaded by mechanical ducts. Light reflects off the white perforated metal decking from fluorescent fixtures positioned upside down on the bottom flange of the joists. Continuing the industrial aesthetic on the exterior are white standing-seam metal walls above the poured-in-place concrete base. The juxtaposition of metal and glass, orthogonal and angular, and openness and enclosure ameliorate a corner of an otherwise monolithic campus.

LEFT: MAIN LIVING SPACE HAS UNINTERRUPTED
VIEWS OF LOPEZ SOUND.

BELOW: SECTION SHOWS ENTRY BRIDGE TO MAIN
LIVING SPACE ON SECOND FLOOR.

Novotny Cabin

Decatur Island, Washington 1990

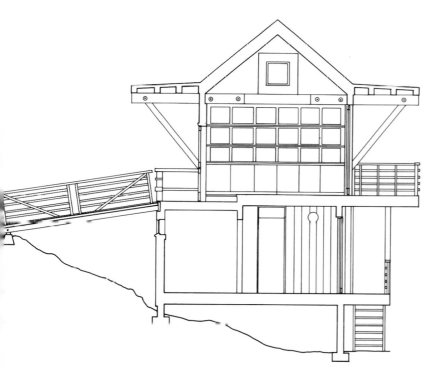

This Decatur Island retreat shares Gorton Bounds' 49
compact form, transparency, and exposed structure,
but is more animated due to the shape of its roof.
Referred to as the "black hat" by islanders, the house
is composed of a series of wood trusses supporting six-
foot-deep overhangs on the east and west sides, which
reduce glare on the glass for better views. These wing-
like projections serve the same function as the flaps of
forest fire watchtowers and recall their iconic profile.

The 840-square-foot cabin sits among Douglas fir and
red-barked madrona trees on the edge of a cliff overlooking Puget Sound. Because of this placement out
from the slope, an entry bridge spans from grade to
the main living space on the second floor. Windows
encircle this treetop aerie making the most of views
across Thatcher Pass to Lopez and Orcas Islands. As
with all of Miller/Hull's work, the relationship to the
outside is key in the design. Here layers of mullions
and struts underscore the dematerialization of the
exterior wall. The kitchen that runs along one end of

RIGHT: EXPANDED AXONOMETRIC

RIGHT BELOW: SITE PLAN

FAR RIGHT: ROOF BEAMS WERE BARGED TO THE
REMOTE SITE IN SECTIONS, THEN ASSEMBLED.

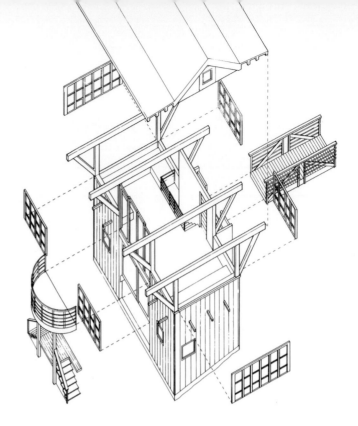

50 the space has open wood-frame cabinets attached to the window mullions for unobstructed views. The four-teen-foot-tall space glows with the fir floors and pine ceilings. In keeping with Decatur Island's resource conservation ethos, the cabin's only source of heat is a wood stove.

The transparent upper level floats the roof above a solid base containing two bedrooms, a study, and a bathroom. The mirror image of the lower level plan is due to the program: two couples built the house together to share on alternating weekends. Each room is only slightly bigger than the built-in double bed, but two large punched windows with views of the water make them seem more spacious. Borrowing from the compactness of a boat cabin, storage space is tucked under the beds, in a crawl space below the floor, and under the built-in seating in the living area.

The structure dominates the architectural expression of the design. Exposed struts and shear connectors support the roof and provide rigidity against seismic forces and severe winds. Construction materials must be barged onto the island, limiting the size of struc-tural members. To address this the structure is com-posite beams shipped in sections and tied together with split ring connectors. The floor beams extend past the exterior wall all the way around the cabin; when spanned by boards they support a window-wash-ing platform. The post-and-beam structure is clad in rough-sawn vertical cedar siding. The cabin is a prime example of the way Miller/Hull manipulates size and scale. As physically compact as possible—the foot-print runs thirteen-by-thirty feet—the cabin's over-sized window frames and overscaled roof increase its visual impact while lessening its intrusion in nature.

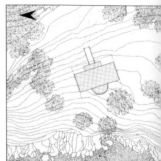

FAR LEFT: GENEROUS OVERHANGS REDUCE
GLASS GLARE.

BELOW LEFT, TOP TO BOTTOM: WEST ELEVATION,
UPPER LEVEL PLAN, LOWER LEVEL PLAN

BELOW: THE CABIN'S ROOF RECALLS THE RAISED
FLAPS OF FOREST FIRE WATCHTOWERS.

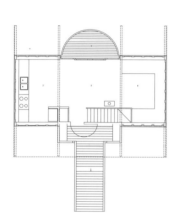

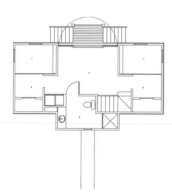

LEFT: PARTIAL AXONOMETRIC

RIGHT: THE STRUCTURE EXTENDS TO FORM A SUN-
SCREEN ON THE WEST.

Boeing Cafeteria

Tukwila, Washington 1991

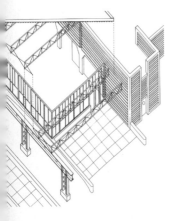

54

At Boeing Field, just south of Seattle, rows of 737s and 757s await delivery to clients around the world. Across the street is the corporate giant's headquarters, part of a secure campus of featureless airplane hangars, research centers, and radar testing facilities between the interstate and the Duwamish River. Miller/Hull's freestanding cafeteria is one of several that serve the large Boeing plant. It is the dining room for workers in two windowless metal buildings—one ten stories and the other five stories tall—across a vast parking lot. The design nods to the form and materials of its utilitarian neighbors while providing a welcome dose of daylight for the employees.

The 10,000-square-foot cafeteria parallels the eastern bank of the river, an industrial waterfront reclaimed as a park for Boeing employees. Miller/Hull developed a series of spaces that become increasingly transparent and articulated as they move from asphalt to water. Fronting the parking lot is a wall of deep-box section corrugated metal siding that extends past both ends of the building by several feet, emphasizing its planar qualities. The vertical seams between panels of the

LEFT: THE TRANSPARENT DINING ROOM PARALLELS
A WATERFRONT PARK.

BELOW: A PORCH SIGNALS THE ENTRY IN THE
OPAQUE EASTERN FAÇADE.

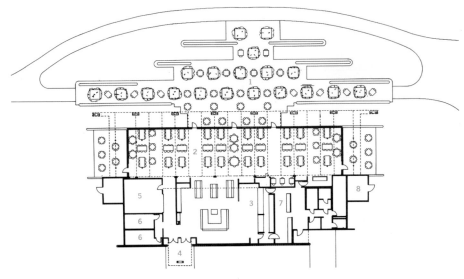

1 **TERRACE** 2 **DINING** 3 **SERVERY** 4 **ENTRY**
5 **DISHWASH** 6 **BATHROOMS** 7 **KITCHEN** 8 **MECHANICAL**

58 horizontal metal siding are articulated with steel angles. The only interruption is for a metal canopy framing a double-height porch. Its singular support is a lattice of steel straps between a pair of wide-flange steel columns, giving a hint of what lies beyond the solid wall.

Layers of corrugated metal walls define a core on the east side of the building containing the food service, kitchen, and dishwashing. Patrons pass through the servery in this enclosed area before emerging into the fourteen-foot-high dining room glazed on three sides. The ceiling's exposed steel bar joists and perforated metal decking are painted white, creating a bright airy space with airplane test models floating overhead. A fine web of steel strap cross bracing between joists adds stiffness while imparting a feeling of weightlessness to the roof. On gray days uplights mounted on poles bounce light off the ceiling. In keeping with Boeing's low-key corporate culture, the room can be partitioned with a pocket door to form a reception center for visiting dignitaries.

To blur the distinction between interior and exterior, the steel joists run from the back wall of the core across the dining room to sit on top of a steel girder outside. The resultant eight-foot-deep overhang on the west side protects the window wall so efficiently that it allows the use of clear rather than tinted glass. Miller/Hull increased the depth of the girder to block more of the low winter sun and then punched a series of portholes in it to decrease its apparent heaviness. A row of the same lattice-like columns found at the entry extends the western edge of the building out into the landscape. The concrete sill is set at tabletop height and is a retaining wall for a raised planter on the outside. To increase the sense of transparency the upper windows are subdivided by steel mullions, breaking up the distracting reflected images that can make glass opaque. The building's transparency, articulation, and texture provide visual relief and human scale in a featureless environment.

LEFT: WATER, TRUCKED INTO THE REMOTE SITE, IS
STORED IN A CISTERN IN THE TOWER.

LEFT BELOW: SITE PLAN

Marquand Retreat

Naches River Valley, Washington 1992

This monk-like retreat nestles in a grassy bowl carved by the Naches River as it winds from the glacial peaks of the Cascade Mountains to the dry Yakima Valley floor. The client, a publisher, camped for a year on the 200-acre site before determining the best place to build: a south facing hillside where elk and deer congregate during the winter. In keeping with his desires, the 450-square-foot project is not a full-fledged house, but rather a permanent shelter, a step up from camping. The cabin's concrete-block walls and corrugated metal roofing withstand wildfires, melding utilitarian decisions with Miller/Hull's low-tech modern aesthetic.

The client chose not to disrupt the pristine landscape with utility lines, and so the cabin has no electricity. Instead, the owner relies on kerosene lamps, a wood stove, and a picnic cooler. Water is trucked into a 500-gallon cistern in a detached concrete-block tower in back of the cabin and gravity fed to the toilet and shower. This tower becomes the anchoring element for the design. A strip of roof engages one edge of the tower then floats over the cabin to tie the two elements together visually. The roof projects another fourteen feet on the south protecting the main opening from the sun with a deep porch.

Daylight penetrates the interior from clerestory windows positioned between the two layers of roof. The ceiling's heavy-timber beams and wood decking warm up the spartan interior's polished concrete floor and exposed light-buff concrete block walls. Since the exterior walls would have had to have been much thicker if furred out to accommodate insulation, the weekend retreat is uninsulated and does not meet the energy code requirements for a residence. For permitting purposes it falls under the category of agricultural buildings—an appropriate designation since the design draws inspiration from farm and industrial buildings in the area.

61

BELOW: CORRUGATED METAL ROOF AND CONCRETE
BLOCK WALLS RESIST WILDFIRES.

RIGHT: GLAZED AND SCREENED PANELS SLIDE HORI-
ZONTALLY OVER THE ENTRY PORTAL.

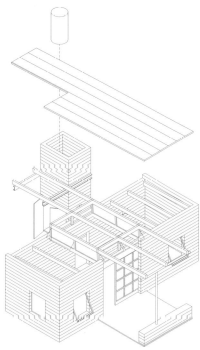

Even within the solidity of this scheme Miller/Hull 65
manages a startling degree of openness with a ten-by-
ten foot portal opening south. Two large panels—one
glazed and the other screened—share the same track
along the length of the house allowing the client to
slide them horizontally for varying degrees of enclosure. When he reluctantly heads back to Seattle, a
metal rolling door pulls down over the main entry and
metal panels secure the wood-frame windows. Usually,
the door is wide open and the polished concrete floor
flows uninterrupted from the interior to the exterior to
stop at a low concrete block wall supporting a single,
off-center column holding up the porch. Together
these spare architectural elements frame a mesmeriz-
ing view of the river valley beyond.

University of Washington Coaches Boat House

Seattle, Washington 1993

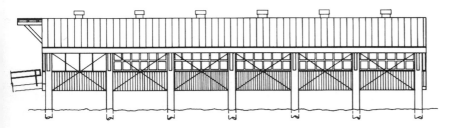

66

The University of Washington's physical education and sports complex stretches along the western edge of Lake Washington in Seattle. Tucked behind the fifty-five-thousand-seat Husky stadium is the university's rowing facility on the marshy shores of Union Bay. Twice daily students carry sleek sixty-foot long racing shells into the water from a low wooden dock. Coaches follow in outboard motor boats from a launch house over the water. In contrast to the blocky, undistinguished building storing the racing shells, the low-slung vault of Miller/Hull's coach house evokes northern European barges—or closer to home—Lake Union houseboats, but with a modernist twist.

The design reflects a stringent sixteen-foot shoreline height restriction—measured from the low point of a two-foot seasonal change in water level. The project's gentle arch allows the building to fall within the height limit without appearing compressed. Another challenge is the location in a bog with load-bearing peat sixty feet below the waterline. It is impossible to

70 drive timber piles that distance and keep them straight, so Miller/Hull used the building envelope, both structurally and conceptually, to bundle the piles together and pull them into vertical alignment. In combination with fine steel rods cross bracing between piers, the system is so effective that no additional diagonal piles are required to stabilize it.

From the landside, the coaches' entry is across a gangplank and under a projecting heavy-timber canopy. Inside, a series of glue-laminated timber arches define six structural bays. The interior docks rise and fall with fluctuations in the water level. Aluminum and glass-paneled garage doors fill five bays and roll up to open the north elevation for boat access. As an economical glazing system the same garage doors infill the bays along the south but are inoperable. On both sides wood struts kick up at the mid-point of each pier to support a roof overhang refracting light off the surface of the water and onto the curved ceiling to modulate the utilitarian interior.

The design contrasts the refined and the raw. The taut machined surface of the standing seam-metal roof plays against the irregular splintered surface of the piers. The hefty proportions of the timber piers, wood struts, and eaves board contrast with the light grid of aluminum mullions and glazing. Aluminum channels mark the seams between the medium-density fiberboard panels that add rigidity at the narrow ends of the structure. The portholes on these elevations nod to the waterfront but their size and location are a graphic element in the composition. The project's gentle vault and repetitious bays make a pictorial reflection among the lily pads and reeds.

Girvin Cabin

Decatur Island, Washington 1994

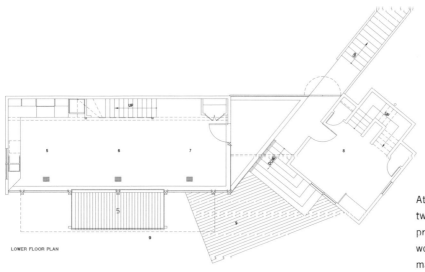

LOWER FLOOR PLAN

1 KITCHEN 2 DINING ROOM
3 LIVING ROOM 4 STUDIO 5 DECK

At 1,950 square feet, this year-round retreat is almost twice the size of Miller/Hull's earlier Decatur Island projects. Although the house is not a cabin-in-the-woods, the design's direct relationship to nature makes it an ideal compromise between camping tent and suburban residence. The client—a family of four—wanted a weekend house as simple as the local fishing sheds. Miller/Hull's crisp and clipped detailing updates the vernacular with a modernist sensibility. The house also marks a new direction for the firm, as it began to experiment with spaces created between volumes.

A string of transitional spaces link a pedestrian access road along the upper edge of the site to a private deck below, cantilevered out over the water. The house turns its back toward the outside world, except for a glass-roofed entry between the main house and a detached studio and guesthouse. This double-height

73

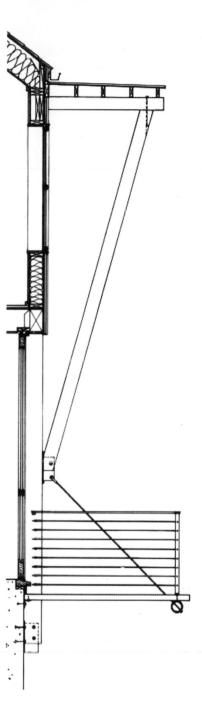

FAR LEFT: GLASS DOORS SLIDE OPEN TO THE LIVING AND
DINING SPACE.

LEFT: WALL SECTION AND DETAIL OF BRACKET SUPPORTING
THE PORCH STRUTS AND CANTILEVERED DECK

OVERLEAF: THE MAIN HOUSE PARALLELS THE SHORELINE;
THE GUESTHOUSE FACES A NEIGHBORING ISLAND.

porch is the main vertical link through the site. The   **75**
long narrow bar of the house parallels the south-facing
shoreline, while the studio angles forty-five degrees
toward a neighboring island. The cranked geometry of
the walls combines with a roof pitched up and out
toward the water and steps cascading down the site to
create a dramatic outdoor space. A wood and glass
garage door slides horizontally out of the way for a
clear opening through the site. Closed it encloses a
protected place out of the wind.

On the main house the slate-gray board-and-batten
siding is narrow, on the guesthouse it is wider—a subtle change in scale that ties them together while
emphasizing their distinctness. The first floor of the
main house is a single room combining kitchen, dining, and living area. The southern face is glass with
two six-by-nine-foot glazed doors that slide aside creating an outdoor room on the edge of a cliff. Heads
and sills are concealed above the ceiling and below
the floor to facilitate an uninterrupted flow of space

LEFT: EARLY SKETCHES

RIGHT: A GLASS-ROOFED EXTERIOR STAIR SLIPS
BETWEEN THE MAIN HOUSE AND STUDIO.

78

from outside to inside. Along the northern edge of the living room a bookcase conceals a stairway up to the master bedroom, two bathrooms, and a children's bedroom with built-in beds. Their windows can stay wide open during rain showers due to the generous overhang above. In the detached studio a narrow stair wraps a bookcase on the way up to a guestroom on the second floor. To fit a bathroom in the compact space, a toilet and shower are behind sandblasted glass doors on either side of the stair.

The detailing of the house is functional and elegant. The attenuated proportion and oblique angle of the wood porch struts mimic the surrounding madrona trees. Overhead the struts support a corrugated metal roof protecting windows on the second floor, but they also extend down so they are visible from inside the first floor—further blurring the boundary between inside and out. At the concrete foundation wall the struts are spliced and bolted to a vertical steel fin, which allows rain to drain away from the wood, preventing rot. Bolted to the bottom of the steel fins are steel rods holding up the edge of a cantilevered deck. The deck's edge beam is a galvanized steel tube with slim steel bars welded on top for balustrades. Combined with the thinness of steel cable railing, the guardrail disappears against the view across Brigantine Bay to Trump Island.

Garfield Community Center

Seattle, Washington 1994

80 Garfield Community Center sits at the intersection of two major thoroughfares in the Central District—a "low-income" residential area between downtown Seattle and Lake Washington. Across one street are a gas station and cluster of shops; the 1902 Colonial Revival-style Horace Mann Elementary School faces it across the other. The corner, a hangout in the past associated with drug dealing and guns, is one that some had given up on—as symbolized by the bunker mentality of the battened concrete walls surrounding a 1970s indoor public pool to the south. In contrast, Miller/Hull's design creates a new neighborhood landmark by anchoring an amorphous city corner in an unexpected way.

Miller/Hull split the 20,000-square-foot community center into two distinct volumes wrapping the corner. The bulk of the gymnasium parallels the street on the west and sits perpendicular to a narrow bar containing community meeting rooms on the north. The space in-between the volumes is a circulation spine connecting a small corner plaza to sports fields behind the building. Inside, the jumbo brick continues around the volumes from the exterior, turning the corridor into a colorful internal street. The gym's standing-seam metal roof follows the ridge of the trusses spanning the basketball court; the slight hip on each end reduces its large mass. The long bar of the meeting rooms is taller than required to bring its scale in line with the gym. Slices of window cut through the north façade, creating freestanding block panels visually tied together by a muscular flat arch of roof. By breaking down the massing, continuing exterior materials inside, and cutting through the facade Miller/Hull creates an open, permeable building.

The project's main entry is on a short cross axis through the narrow north block of meeting rooms, leading to a multipurpose room on the south. Where it crosses the long east to west circulation, columns mark the intersection with a halo of light from pyramidal skylights concealed above the open wood slat ceiling.

2323

E THAT HELPS ANOTHER HELPS HIMSELF ✝✝ PEACE C

CS IN PROPORTION TO OUR IG

RAISE A

This also highlights the entrance to the multipurpose room—the heart of the building—sitting in the crook of the "L" defined by the gym and meeting rooms. Enclosed on its open edge by a wall of windows, the space has a full catering kitchen for receptions and community dinners. Glazed roll-up garage doors open the room to a patio; the patio, protected by a floating metal canopy that blurs the boundary of the room, provides additional entertainment space. In contrast to its urban presence on the corner, the back of the community center presents an irregular and informal face to the sports fields.

Glazed roll-up garage doors in two corners of the gymnasium bring light in and give a sense of the activity inside to the street. Randomly placed glass blocks bring in pinpoints of light, easing the massiveness of the brick wall. Daylight also trickles in from skylights filtered by louvers and fins to control glare. Throughout the project, there is an emphasis on natural lighting and ventilation and sustainability. Wherever possible the building's materials utilize recycled wallboard, insulation, and paint.

BELOW: PLAN, SHOWING RELATIONSHIP TO STREET
CORNER.

RIGHT: SLICES CUT THROUGH THE NARROW BAR OF
MEETING ROOMS TO INVITE IN THE NEIGHBORHOOD.

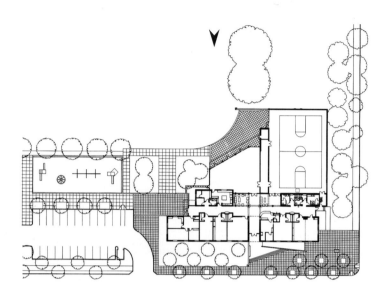

84   The random mix of teal, orange, and gray bricks set in the jumbo brick walls marks the beginning of Miller/Hull's exploration of color in their work. The suggestion for color came from community meetings held during the design process. This input was key in building local support and ties to the neighborhood. Public art, from the iconic figures in niches in the hallway to the collection of quotations inscribed in the risers of the plaza stair, is fully incorporated into the building design. Part of Seattle's one-percent-for-art program, it is of symbolic importance to the community. The community center extends an open invitation to the neighborhood, making the place a fulcrum for revitalization.

BY FORCE, IT CAN ONLY BE ACHIEVED BY UNDERSTANDING ✦ A CHILD MISEDUCATED IS A CHILD LOST ✦
ICE IS NO LONGER BETWEEN VIOLENCE AND NONVIOLENCE, IT IS EITHER NONVIOLENCE OR NONEXISTENCE ✦
ROTHERS OR PERISH TOGETHER AS FOOLS ✦ LISTEN TO THE SONG OF LIFE ✦ WISDOM IS BETTER THAN STRENGTH
E COMMUNITY ✦ NOTHING CAN DIM THE LIGHT WHICH SHINES WITHIN ✦ TECHNOLOGY DOES NOT TEACH REVERENCE

LEFT: THE DESIGN RECALLS THE LOCAL VERNACULAR
OF SIMPLE SHEDS AND TIMBER MILLS.

BELOW: SOUTH ELEVATION

Olympic College
Shelton, Washington 1995

With an animated volume, monolithic roof, and deft handling of materials Miller/Hull achieves a physical presence for Olympic College in Shelton worthy of its symbolic role in a struggling timber-working community. Before the college was built young people left town to get a secondary education—often never to return. Only through donations of cedar siding and glu-lam beams from one timber company, a free wooded 27-acre site from another company, and services from several local businesses, was the economically pressed town of Shelton able to build this satellite community college. Of the $1.4 million construction budget, over $500,000 was raised by the town and matched by Olympic College; the balance came from donation of services and projects. Miller/Hull wove these disparate resources into a coherent whole, to create a design that in 1998 won a National AIA Honor Award.

Environmental and budget concerns formed critical elements of Miller/Hull's campus master plan, deter-

LEFT: FACULTY OFFICES OCCUPY THE EXTERIOR
CIRCULATION PATHS LINKING CLASSROOMS.

BELOW: A COLLEGE NESTLED IN THE PACIFIC
NORTHWEST WOODS

mining the buildings' locations and their compact
footprints. Located on a flat swath of land, the long,
narrow form of Phase I cuts the site, organizing it in
one simple step. To the north, a bio-filtration swale
treats storm water run-off from the parking lot and
creates a landscape buffer between building and cars.
On the south, an informal campus "quadrangle" is
delineated by the building, the hills, and woods.
Phase II, planned for the western edge of the site parallel to the main road, will further define the heart of
the campus.

While the limited budget required a modest form, the
expansive roof gives the project a larger presence than
its 8,000 square feet might suggest. Facing the main
road, the roof shelters a double-height porch supported by a dramatic "V" of steel pipes that creates an
identifiable public image for the college. Along the
quad on the south side of the building, the roof cantilevers twelve feet out over the exterior circulation
between classrooms. Faculty offices, developed as

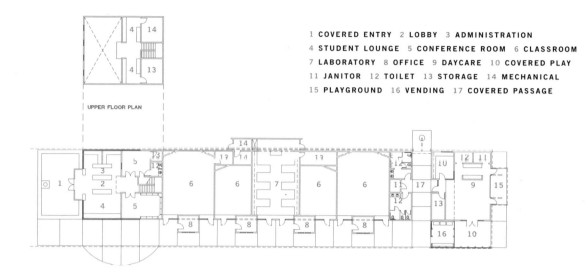

UPPER FLOOR PLAN

1 COVERED ENTRY 2 LOBBY 3 ADMINISTRATION
4 STUDENT LOUNGE 5 CONFERENCE ROOM 6 CLASSROOM
7 LABORATORY 8 OFFICE 9 DAYCARE 10 COVERED PLAY
11 JANITOR 12 TOILET 13 STORAGE 14 MECHANICAL
15 PLAYGROUND 16 VENDING 17 COVERED PASSAGE

discrete volumes, punctuate the classroom wall, articulating this elevation and providing a more intimate scale. Over the daycare center at the rear of the building the roof slopes in the opposite direction, up toward the woods, giving it a separate identity. The two roofs meet at an oversized scupper, with chains salvaged from a local naval yard hanging down into a welded steel catch basin below. Rainwater collects and flows down the chains like a waterfall.

At the daycare center, a wood latticework covered with translucent panels screens a portion of the exterior walkway to protect outdoor play on rainy days. On sunny days a bright yellow overhead door rolls up to extend the two-story classroom into the playground.

Interior spaces are as compact and flexible as a ship's. Classrooms also accommodate community and civic functions. The main lobby contains administrative offices, a student lounge, and a resource center. At dusk the lobby's large windows, combined with uplighting on the underside of the roof, make the building glow like a camp lantern in the woods. Round

windows in the end elevations and in the faculty's office doors add to the project's buoyant, pop art sensibility.

Miller/Hull achieved variety within a limited material palette by juxtaposing the textures of natural and manufactured wood products. Stained horizontal beveled wood siding is at the building's base. Above are manufactured wood panels painted a saturated puce green, which is accented by silky cinnamon on the exterior doors. Joints between panels, comprised of overscaled wood battens, create a vertical rhythm. Metal hexagonal nuts—the panel fasteners—were left unpainted for added texture. The articulated detailing, contrasting textures, and vibrant colors transform the simple shed of local timber mills into a modern design.

91

Passenger-Only Ferry Terminal

Seattle, Washington—Unbuilt 1995

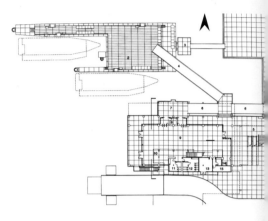

92 On Seattle's bustling downtown waterfront, Colman Dock is the main terminal for the large ferries that traffic weekday commuters—on foot, on bicycles, or in cars—across Puget Sound from island residences to city jobs. Miller/Hull's design for a 7,500-square-foot terminal was designed to accommodate two or three small passenger-only ferries to Vashon and other neighboring islands. The project was shelved when the ferry system decided to expand the number of vessels beyond the capacity of the tight site. Even though unbuilt, the design is interesting for Miller/Hull's handling of complex circulation patterns and its abstract maritime aesthetic.

The proposed terminal projects into Elliott Bay on the north side of Colman Dock and shares its upper level concourse. Pedestrians arrive via a sky bridge that begins at grade on First Avenue several blocks away and, as the city slopes down to the waterfront, crosses above busy streets to the upper level of the termi-

nal. Passengers walk down stairs and escalators to ticketing in a double-height lobby and then over a gangplank to a floating dock. The project's large shed roof angles down to trace the flow of passengers then cantilevers up to cover a waiting area and as a gesture to incoming ferries. Concrete pilings continue up from under the water through the building to support a series of eight exposed steel king post trusses. A glass curtain wall allows uninterrupted views of the bay. In a bar on the mezzanine level, San Francisco artist Paul Koss designed a large video display of images of boat traffic on Elliott Bay linked to a nautical radar antenna on top of the building. Outside, a clock tower (housing an elevator) and a viewing deck on a mooring dolphin are part of a new public space along the waterfront.

LEFT: DRAWING OF PUGET SOUND CONCOURSE
AND DOCK

RIGHT: MODELS OF SHED ROOF ANGLING DOWN FROM
UPPER-LEVEL CONCOURSE TO THE WATER.

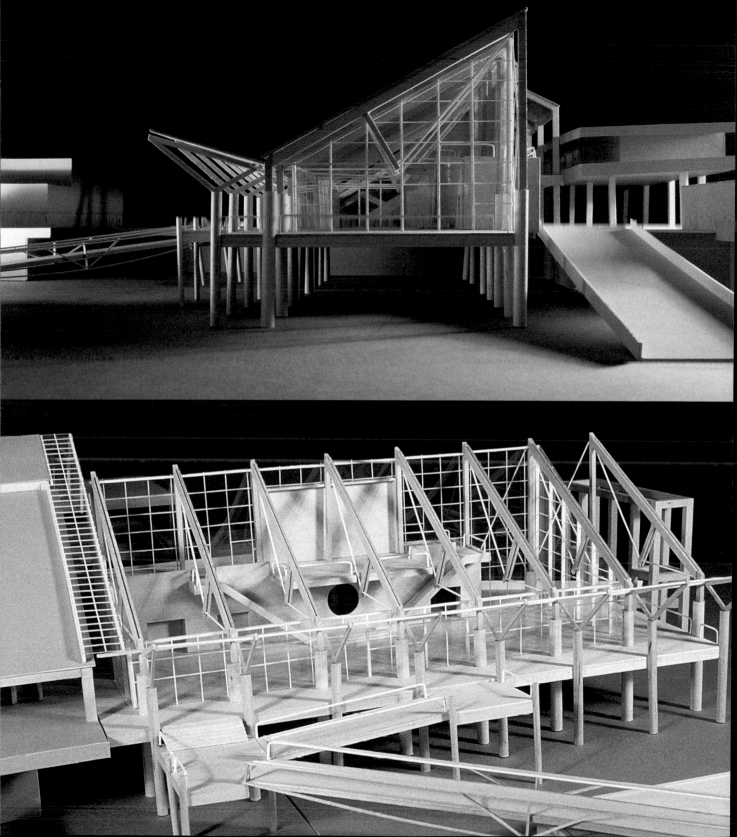

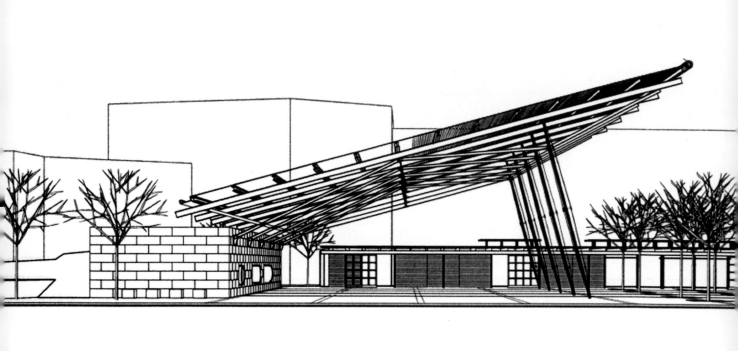

LEFT TOP AND BOTTOM: OVERSCALED ROOF, LINEAR
BAR, AND GLOBE DEFINE THE PLAZA.

BELOW: AIR DRAWN OVER A POOL AND THROUGH PIPES
IS COOLED, THEN DISCHARGED UNDER THE SHED ROOF.

Environmental Pavilion Summer Olympics

Atlanta, Georgia—Unbuilt 1996

Miller/Hull's reputation for sustainable architecture led to an invitation to design the Environmental Pavilion for the 1996 Summer Olympics in Atlanta. A shortfall in corporate sponsorship prevented its realization, yet it is valuable to present because of the exaggerated roof—a compelling voice for green design. It also draws an audience by creating a cool refuge from the heat along a major pedestrian promenade linking athletic events.

The overscaled shed roof is one of four elements that defines an exterior plaza including a straw bale berm on the west, a bar containing an international food court on the north, and a globe containing a conference center on the east. The roof, a combination of recycled steel beams and paralam wood joists, shades an area for exhibits and tables for the cafe. Air is drawn over a circular pool and through pre-cast concrete pipes embedded in the straw bale retained earth berm. The mass of the berm cools the air as it travels the length of the pipes and it then discharges under the roof to naturally cool the space. Photovoltaic panels on the roof power the facility including a large projection screen along the promenade displaying environmental messages and updates on the Games. A spiral staircase paired with an elevator takes visitors up into the globe of recycled nylon fabric over a steel structure that floats over the plaza in a grove of trees. Inside, multimedia presentations project on the curved ceiling. For a longer life than the Olympics, the roof is demountable for reuse as a bandstand or picnic shelter in a city park.

97

NW Federal Credit Union

Seattle, Washington 1996

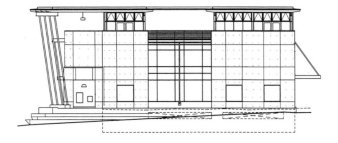

98

In the NW Federal Credit Union, located on Seattle's northern periphery, Miller/Hull combined sustainable principles with market-driven considerations. A stone's throw from the interstate, the site is screened from a cemetery by a row of cedar and pine trees. The project's grand porch gestures to the community and creates an independent identity for a federal employee service typically subsumed in government buildings. At 40,000 square feet it includes a branch bank, administrative offices, and tenant space into which the credit union will expand. The design's scale, articulation, and transparency define a new type of urbanism among the detritus of shopping malls, undistinguished office parks, and fast food restaurants.

The long, narrow building's main axis runs east to west, facilitating cross ventilation and the penetration of daylight into the interior. For visibility from the road, the branch bank is on the east end of the building. A window wall shaded by a floating metal roof creates a three-story porch for the bank and distinguishes it from the office space. The roof edge projects at an angle away from the facade, and a colonnade of cant-

LEFT: SUSTAINABLE FEATURES INCLUDE DAYLIGHT-
ING, ENERGY-EFFICIENT MECHANICAL SYSTEMS, AND
RECYCLED MATERIALS.

BELOW: SITE DIAGRAM ILLUSTRATING SUSTAINABLE
PRINCIPLES

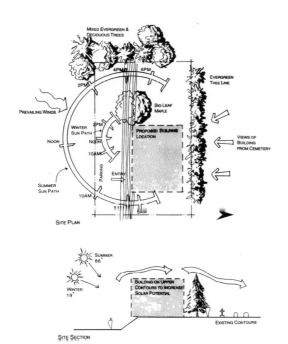

ed steel columns steps out to follow it to emphasize the entry. On the east elevation, concrete walls bracket a two-story window wall and extend up to the parapet, creating a public scale. Wrapping the office block is a cast-in-place concrete base with a plaster wall at the second floor. Pilasters mark the structural bays and extend up to the roof; their termination creates a crenellated parapet infilled with metal railing, forming a kind of modern cornice.

The main entry is a two-story lobby between the bank and offices. A super-graphic of a one-dollar bill dominates the wall along a generous staircase connecting the first and second floors. Down the middle of the open office space is a solid core containing functions that need enclosure—private offices, conference areas, and computer rooms—leaving the perimeter open. On the partial third floor are training rooms, showers for bicycle commuters, and an airy south-facing lunchroom and outdoor deck with treetop views of downtown.

The office spaces have high ceilings; exposed lightweight steel truss joists and metal decking painted

white bounce daylight farther inside. Each large, south-facing window has a sunscreen of steel grating set in tube steel frames on the exterior and an interior metal light shelf for glare control and to boost the penetration of daylight. Photo-sensors dim artificial lights when natural light levels are sufficient. To draw out daytime heat and improve indoor air quality, an energy-efficient mechanical system with a night flushing cycle pumps cool evening air through the building while exhausting airborne contaminants. Operable windows on the third floor allow natural ventilation in the training rooms and lunchroom. Throughout the project, embodied energy and recycled content were key issues in the selection of materials; the structural frame is recycled steel, the cast-in-place concrete contains fly ash admixtures, and the gypsum board walls, fiberglass batt insulation, and ceiling tiles all have recycled content. Miller/Hull combines daylighting, energy-efficient mechanical systems, and natural ventilation to reduce the building's energy draw thirty percent below stringent state requirements. All this in turn makes a generic project much more expressive.

101

LEFT: INSIDE, A LIGHT SHELF BOUNCES DAYLIGHT INTO THE OFFICE SPACE

BELOW: EXTERIOR WALL SECTION AT SUNSCREEN

RIGHT: SUNSCREEN OF TUBE STEEL AND METAL GRATING.

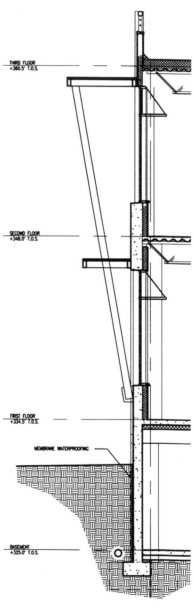

THIRD FLOOR
+360.5' T.O.S.

SECOND FLOOR
+348.0' T.O.S.

FIRST FLOOR
+334.5' T.O.S.

MEMBRANE WATERPROOFING

BASEMENT
+325.0' T.O.S.

Lake Washington School District
Resource Center

Redmond, Washington 1997

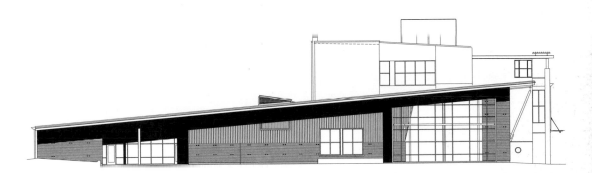

With the new headquarters for the Lake Washington School District, Miller/Hull tackled the dilemma of placing a public building in the only identifiable center of a suburban community: an open air shopping center. Connected to Seattle by a floating bridge across Lake Washington, Redmond Town Center knits 1.5-million square feet of retail, offices, and hotel space into the old main street area by extending the street grid and the pedestrian scale. For the progressive school district, the location is ideal for forging connections to the community, and for providing space for the Parent Teacher Association, school board meetings, a library for teachers and parents, and centralized administration. It is also the electronic information hub for the district's student run-website and accompanying computer training classrooms. With a nod to the shopping center's guidelines, Miller/Hull bends the rules with a concrete frame, floating planes of brick, and an articulated skin to distinguish a civic building in the midst of a mall.

Miller/Hull organizes the 55,000-square-foot project into two distinct volumes that reflect the differences in program and location on the site. Fronting the main shopping street along the south is an urban three-story office block that consolidates the school district's administrative staff. Along the west is a wedge of corrugated metal siding and window wall containing the training area and a commons space that connects it to the administration block. The vast slope of standing-seam metal roof begins low off a modest entry on the north end and rises to a double-height porch on the south to fit the one level piece up against the three-story block.

The main entry is under the front porch off the main street and into a double-height commons area. The brick cladding the exterior unwraps here revealing the concrete columns and the second level administrative area above the lobby. A grand stair and balcony invite visitors to the upper floor district offices. On the first

LEFT: THE OFFICE BLOCK ALIGNS WITH THE STREET;
THE TRAINING ROOM WEDGE FITS AMONG TREES.

RIGHT: AN OPEN STAIRWAY TO SECOND-FLOOR
DISTRICT OFFICES

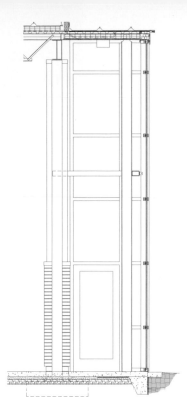

FAR LEFT: TRAINING ROOMS, CONNECTED BY AN
INTERIOR STREET, HAVE GENEROUS OUTDOOR VIEWS.

LEFT: CURTAIN WALL SECTION

LEFT BELOW: SITE PLAN

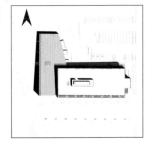

109

floor, a front desk and a library for teachers and parents sit in the open corner of the administrative block with the commons beyond. It is a vibrant interior street where multiple activities for the public, parents, school board, teachers, and students come together. Along the west wall are multi-purpose and conference rooms. Wood-clad cabanas containing meeting rooms and a kitchen punctuate the window-wall on the east. A glazed garage door rolls up to allow the lobby to flow out onto a patio and a stand of century-old cedars.

In the articulation of the layers of the administrative block's skin, Miller/Hull gives the storefronts typical of the region's neighborhood shopping districts a modernist twist. The composition of the facade is straightforward: a pedestrian-oriented ground floor with extensive glazing and a protective rain awning, a solid middle zone punctuated by windows, and a cornice at the roofline. The difference lies in the detailing. The depth of the red brick—the primary materials of the center—is revealed at corners and edges, emphasizing that it is a plane hung from an exposed concrete frame and not a bearing wall. A light steel and glass rain canopy balances on a large steel tube, which runs the length of the storefront and is hung on fine steel rods. The large openings in the brick skin center on the structural frame, revealing a concrete column with windows on either side. These openings alternate with small yellow-framed operable windows across the front elevation. At the third floor, the facade steps back to a metal and glass mansard with a steel trellis, providing texture and interest at the roofline. Through the detailing of the exterior wall, Miller/Hull achieves maximum articulation in minimum depth.

Tahoma National Cemetery

Kent, Washington 1997

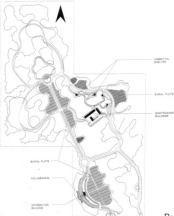

110

Burials at national cemeteries are highly mechanized processes. Services take place in open-air committal shelters and afterwards forklifts position three or four caskets at a time in underground vaults. Within these parameters Miller/Hull creates in the Tahoma National Cemetery a distinctively regional cemetery, by orienting the design toward woods, wetlands, and views. A ceremonial drive created by landscape architects Jongejan Gerrard McNeal organizes the 160-acre forested site along an axis, linking a formal flag plaza to the 14,410-foot summit of nearby Mount Rainier. A connection to nature is evident throughout the cemetery, mitigating the inherent dichotomy in a project that is the most overtly symbolic of Miller/Hull's work and also the most restrictive programmatically.

LEFT: THE COMMITTAL SHELTERS SIT AMONG LARGE FIRS.

BELOW: A LARGE WINDOW PROVIDES A BACKDROP FOR
FUNERAL SERVICES.

Tahoma National Cemetery is twenty-five miles south
of Seattle in an area where farmland is turning over to
housing developments. The gateway into the cemetery
begins on axis with the flag pavilion but curves to the
left toward a public information pavilion. The 1,230-
square-foot structure divides into two symmetrical
pieces—one transparent, the other opaque—under a
gable metal roof. On the south end steel sash windows
enclose a waiting area seismically braced by steel
cables and anchored on a low stone wall. On the north,
the volcanic stone walls enclose public restrooms. An
open-air breezeway links the two spaces and contains
a computer terminal to locate a service, grave, or urn.
Aligned with the building's cross axis through the
breezeway are three columbariums. The concrete niches with marble covers will eventually contain the cre-
mated remains of 13,000 veterans.

BELOW: SITE PLAN SHOWING THE INFORMATION
PAVILION WITH THE COLUMBARIUMS.

RIGHT: BASALT FOR THE PAVILION'S WALLS WAS
QUARRIED FROM MOUNT RAINIER.

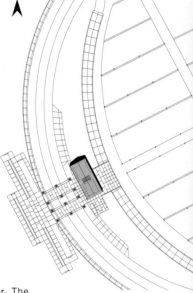

114   On the east side of the information pavilion is the cortege assembly area, and from there the road links onto a traffic circle at the southern end of the ceremonial axis that terminates at the flag pavilion to the north. On either side of the drive, the edge of the woods expands and contracts around meadows containing 74,000 gravesites. A series of unobtrusive control markers orient visitors to specific graves.

From the flag plaza, the drive loops east through the dense forest to two of the four planned committal shelters. Minimal architectural elements define the open-air structures: a metal gable roof, a stone wall, and a steel window screening one end. The window imparts direction to the space, focusing it on a casket, a speaker, or the tranquil view of fir trees beyond. Miller/Hull also uses the window as a way to add another layer of detail and texture to the shelter. The window sits on a low wall of porous black rock quarried on Mount Rainier; it forms a ledge for flowers, photographs, and mementos. The main structure is composed of exposed steel pipe columns and beams with wood rafters and wood decking on top. Outside the pavilion an eight-foot stone wall defines a small support building housing the sound system, utilities, and chair storage. From each area a path leads into the woods inviting personal contemplation. The juxtapositions of transparency and solidity, rough and smooth, the natural and the man-made create a place that is immediate and intimate as well as refined and dignified.

LEFT: TRANSPARENT PORTHOUSE HAS UNOBSTRUCTED
VIEWS OF EXTERIOR INSPECTION AREAS.

BELOW: EARLY DIAGRAMS

Point Roberts Border Station

Point Roberts, Washington 1997

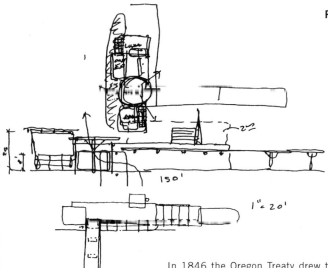

In 1846 the Oregon Treaty drew the Canadian border along the 49th parallel cutting off the southern tip of British Columbia and making Point Roberts United States territory. To reach this four-square-mile appendix of land, U.S. citizens must enter Canada, drive around Boundary Bay, and then re-enter at the Point Roberts border station. Of the peninsula's 12,000 full-time residents, seventy percent are Canadians who commute daily to jobs in Vancouver. When increasing traffic overwhelmed the existing 1950s pre-fabricated booth, the General Services Administration decided to make its replacement the first border station commissioned under a new design excellence program to raise the quality of federal architecture: the project won a National AIA Honor Award in 2000. Miller/Hull created a steel-and-glass gateway as equally at ease in the forest as it is at projecting a federal presence.

The 12,000-square-foot project is 200 feet south of the border across a small lawn from the boxy, stucco Canadian checkpoint. It has three distinct program elements—a porthouse, a main inspection area, and a secondary inspection area—each with specific requirements regarding visibility into and from other spaces. Border agents must be able to survey the two outdoor inspection areas from the porthouse. The station must also, however, house secure areas within the porthouse cloaked from public view. Miller/Hull translated these requirements into three separate spaces—a solid bar, a transparent observation space, and two large canopies—that have varying degrees of transparency.

The porthouse is the main interior space containing offices, secure areas, and a public information area with a basement below. The east facade of the bar is the building's most opaque, clad in wood-batten siding with a few punched openings and containing private offices, holding cells, and other secure areas. Paralleling Tyee Drive, it screens traffic waiting to cross at the Canadian border station. Running along the porthouse's west face is an enclosed steel and glass porch housing open office space, a desk from

117

RIGHT TOP AND BOTTOM: WEST AND EAST ELEVATIONS

CENTER: MAIN INSPECTION AREA IS PERPENDICULAR
TO THE PORTHOUSE; A SECONDARY CANOPY ANGLES
TO THE SOUTH.

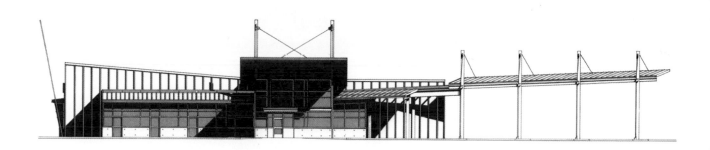

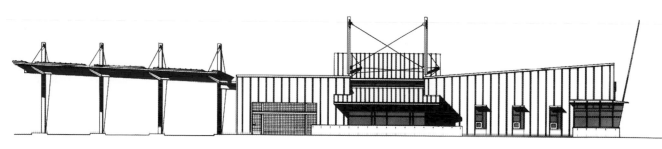

which agents monitor the cars outside, and a lobby for the public. Bicyclists crossing the border dismount and come inside to speak with an agent. Perpendicular to the porthouse is the canopy covering the main inspection area. A pull-off area for further inspection lies under a separate canopy that angles off the end of the porthouse, allowing agents to monitor it from there.

The two cable-stayed steel canopies dominate the design. A pair of masts strung with steel cable pick up the 100-foot cantilever of the main canopy as it emerges from the carapace of the porthouse and soars up to the highest point over the outside truck lane. To resist uplift, cables stretch down from the canopy and moor it to two bollards at an inspection booth. As the canopy crosses over the top of the porthouse it notches to engage the two disparate forms. This creates an open zone bisecting the porthouse containing the lobby and a radio communication center before breaking through the back wall into a lunchroom. The secondary

free-standing canopy is suspended from a row of steel piers by a triangulation of cables that picks up its cantilevered edges and then tie it to a steel plate at the base.

The form of the station arises directly from the program, instead of an overarching or preconceived idea. The design's strength lies in the disjunction between requirements. Steel "K"-bracing and skylights stitch the split between the canopies' structure and the wood porthouse together, creating a layered, transparent space. The quest for structural rationalism leaves no room for overstatement: the proportions of the beams, the placement of cables, and the detailing of the connections are expressive without crossing into mannerism. The layers of steel structure and glass define an open structure that links transparency to a democratic society.

121

LEFT: WALL SECTION AT METAL SLIDING DOOR

RIGHT: CLERESTORY WINDOWS AND ROOF MONITORS
BRING DAYLIGHT INTO THE GARAGE.

North Kitsap
Transportation Center

Poulsbo, Washington 1997

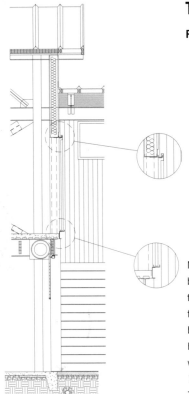

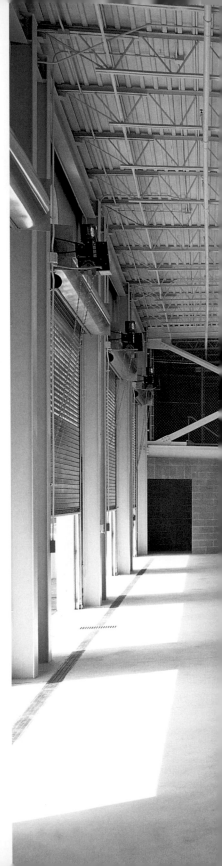

122

Miller/Hull's school bus maintenance facility is a hub-bub of activity on the Kitsap Peninsula just south of the tiny town of Kingston. In rural areas like this, bus facilities form the backdrop for the daily interactions between parents, the director of transportation, and bus dispatchers concerning kids, schedules, and the weather. At the same time, the Kitsap School District's 150 buses are washed, maintained, and parked here. Typically, bus facilities are big boxes with space for an office tacked on the side, but Miller/Hull acknowledges the building's role in community life with a design that is utilitarian yet civic minded.

The 20,000-square-foot building sits in a meadow surrounded by trees, a half-mile from the rocky shores of Puget Sound. The building's straightforward L-shaped plan is animated by a series of sloping roof planes that flutter over the five-acre site. By alternating the direction of their slope, the large shed roofs underscore the dividing line that separates people and buses on the long, narrow property. The subtle manipulation of the building section breaks down the mass and brings natural light deep inside.

124 A front porch at the south end of the building is the first sight to greet the public and spares them a wade through a sea of asphalt in search of the front door. At the porch's glazed entry, open web steel joists and steel beams continue the structure outside, emphasizing continuity between the interior and exterior. Set into the inexpensive storefront window system are hopper windows for natural ventilation. Miller/Hull used the operable panels' wider mullions as a compositional element within each storefront system to achieve variety and interest around the building. Inside, an open reception area leads to a cluster of offices, a training room, and a large lunchroom. Tomato-red marmoleum floors warm up the interior's exposed steel structure, metal roof decking, and mechanical ducts. A corrugated metal wall demarcates the heated portion of the building from the garage on the other side.

In the garage, five bus bays—each twenty-feet-wide by sixty-feet-deep—form a large volume high enough to accommodate a school bus raised on a mechanic's lift. Bracketing the garage on either end are specific shops and mechanics' areas with parts storage in mezzanines above. Perpendicular to the north end of the building are three additional bus bays—originally designed as a second phase but built contemporaneous with the first phase—and a covered area for bus washing and fueling. Garages generally tend to be dark and undesirable work environments, but here clerestory windows and roof monitors allow the penetration of natural light into each bus bay. White paint on the exposed structure and metal roof decking reflects light inside. Slots in the roll-up garage doors bring in additional light, and round vents above each door—boosted by a vehicle exhaust system—facilitate air circulation.

The project's materials are durable and inexpensive but the detailing is refined. The most interesting example of this is found in how the project turns the corner from five garage bays to three at the north end. The roof extends to define a fourth bay that overlaps the main volume. Underneath is a large upper window on a one-story block wall. As it turns the corner, the block wall notches down before continuing past to emphasize lightness and transparency. It's a subtle and sophisticated gesture visible to few people but demonstrates Miller/Hull's commitment to design.

ABOVE: ALTERNATING SLOPED ROOF PLANES SUBTLY ANIMATE A UTILITARIAN BUILDING.

BELOW: SECTION THROUGH MAIN GARAGE WITH BUS WASHING FACILITY BEYOND

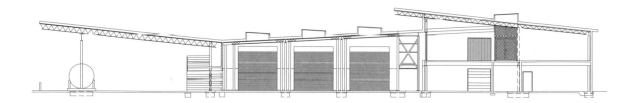

BELOW: AN INTERIOR CORRUGATED METAL WALL
DEMARCATES THE HEATED PORTION OF THE BUILDING.

RIGHT: CHAIN LINK FENCE ENCLOSES A SECOND
FLOOR MECHANICAL SPACE.

LEFT: OUTDOOR CONNECTIONS ARE ESSENTIAL FOR
THE LAB'S ENVIRONMENTALISTS.

OVERLEAF: RAIN ON THE ROOF IS ROUTED INTO
DEMONSTRATION WATER TREATMENT PONDS.

BELOW: EARLY STUDY OF BUILDING SECTION

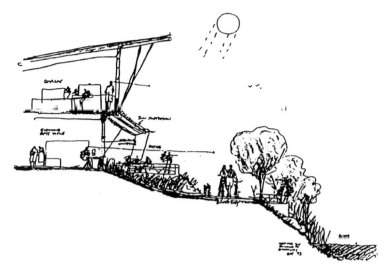

Water Pollution Control Laboratory

Portland, Oregon 1997

Like many cities, Portland's storm-water and sewage system share pipes. During heavy rains they overflow into the Willamette River that snakes through downtown. Miller/Hull's new Water Pollution Control Laboratory for Portland's Bureau of Environmental Services is part of a city-wide program to test, control, and reduce overflow while raising public awareness of storm-water runoff. The project's eleven-acre site is along a ten-mile-long riverside park and under the 400-foot-tall neogothic ramparts of the St. John's suspension bridge. Across the river is a hillside community with an aerial view of the 40,000-square-foot project. In this context, Miller/Hull took the roofscape as the starting point for the design. They considered its scenographic quality while addressing the notorious amount of rooftop mechanical equipment that laboratories require. When it rains the roof is a dramatic demonstration of urban runoff as oversized scuppers pour rainwater into a landscaped treatment pond on the waterside site.

Miller/Hull organized the project in seven long bays that alternate sloped planes with strips of mechanical cores that project up above the roof to conceal rooftop equipment. The bays vary in width, program, and transparency. The first one parallels the river on the west and is the most articulated; it contains open administrative office space, the cafeteria, and large multi-purpose rooms. The roof begins over a grand public porch on the south and slopes up toward the bridge on the north. The second bay is an enclosed two-story service core containing stairs, rest rooms, and private conference rooms. Its vertical volume and flat roof conceal mechanical equipment and provide a visual break between the large sloping plane over the office block and the vast roof over the laboratory. Four adjoining bays contain 15,000-square-feet of laboratory covered by a large roof. It starts low on the south and slopes up to a double-height porch on the north with a textured grid of pyramidal skylights studding the corrugated metal. The last bay on the east end is

129

BELOW: WEST ELEVATION

RIGHT: THE FIRST-FLOOR CANOPY IS HUNG FROM
AND PROPPED UP BY STEEL BRACKETS

OVERLEAF: SKYLIGHTS AND WINDOWS BRING DAY-
LIGHT INTO THE LABORATORY.

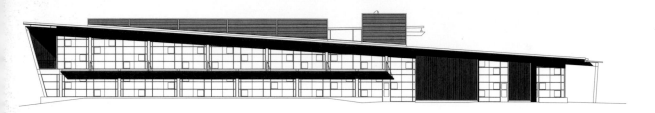

132   a two-story core containing sample receiving areas, lab support spaces, and a loading area on the first floor and mechanical systems for the lab on the second floor. The roof's alternating vertical volumes and horizontal planes echo the supports and spans of the suspension bridge and the exposed steel frame is painted the same grass green.

The building's occupants are environmentalists with an interest in sustainable architecture. Laboratories, however, require careful controls, which make natural ventilation systems impossible. Instead, Miller/Hull focused on the open office space, peppering the black grid of the window wall with a secondary system of bright aluminum operable windows. A green light signals when the chiller is off and the windows can be opened. This glazed western elevation opens to views of the river and is protected by the syncopated rhythm of a brise-soleil. Shading the first floor is a metal grille alternately hung from or propped up by steel kickers, depending on the location of supporting columns staggered above

and below an exposed steel edge beam at the second floor. The exaggerated tectonics of a sunshade at the roof line emphasizes the lightness and layering of the roof construction with a narrow gap between the metal roof decking on cantilevered steel roof rafters before feathering out to the fine metal grille.

In the laboratory Miller/Hull created a loft-like space, with six individual work areas in large nooks off a wide circulation spine. A grid of skylights overhead and large windows on both ends of the common area facilitate the synergy of working toward a shared goal. During the day, visitors view the inner workings of the lab through large windows in a corridor that extends the length of the building and ends at a gangplank over the demonstration filtration pond. In the evening the building can be secured to make the large multipurpose rooms available for community meetings. The laboratory's porches and integration with the waterfront park transform a utilitarian project into an opportunity to educate the public.

BELOW: NORTH ELEVATION

RIGHT: L-SHAPED VISITOR CENTER AND DAY CAMP
DEFINE AN OUTDOOR ROOM.

Discovery Park Visitor Center

Seattle, Washington 1997

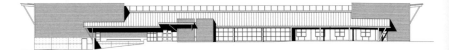

136 In the early 1900s the renowned landscape architects the Olmsted Brothers of Brookline, Massachusetts, eyed the Fort Lawton military base on a bluff overlooking Puget Sound as part of their master plan for Seattle's parks system. It took more than sixty years for their vision to be realized; the 527 acres of tidal beaches, stands of native trees, and meadowlands close to downtown became Discovery Park in 1973. Over the years the army's presence had taken an environmental toll on the land. Miller/Hull's Visitor Center plays a role in the park's restoration, as a place to orient and educate the public. Hikers start here to learn about the park's flora and fauna before heading out on the trails for a glimpse of bald eagles.

The new 11,500-square-foot building sits in the footprint of a demolished army barrack. Miller/Hull defined a south-facing outdoor room by placing two narrow bars perpendicular to each other to form an "L" facing a grassy hillock and wall of pines. The Visitor Center's entry is through the east end of the main bar and into an exhibit area and out to a double-height glazed porch facing the courtyard. Inside, public areas include the Discovery Room for children's orientation, a large multi-purpose room, and a row of classrooms. Offices for docents and naturalists are at the west end of the building. Across the outdoor space is a separate building with a row of flexible rooms housing a children's day camp in the summer and conferences and retreats the rest of the year.

The large shed roof over the visitor's center dominates the design. It begins low on the north facing a small parking lot and climbs to a double-height porch on the south. A pair of two-story cedar-clad volumes bookend the elevation on the east and west. A boxy one-story volume on the front conceals the restrooms and signals the main entry with a floating plane of cantilevered roof. The receding and projecting voids in combination with the roofs recall the layered transparency of forest undergrowth. Visitors follow the rise of the shed roof as they walk under the low eaves on

LEFT: THE WOODEN CEILING GIVES WAY TO TRANSLUCENT
PANELS FROM THE LOBBY TO THE PORCH.

BELOW: PORCH, OPEN AND ENCLOSED THE LENGTH OF
THE BUILDING

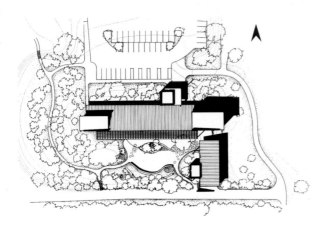

140   the north, through the exhibit space, and out into porch along the back of the building. At the porch the wood roof changes to translucent panels, exposing the wood joists supported by a colonnade of exposed steel structure. A section of the porch at the exhibit space is glazed, creating an indoor/outdoor gathering spot at the trailhead.

The Visitor Center's broad roofs and woodsy material palette recall the national park service buildings that dot the American West, but Miller/Hull's graphic sensibility stakes out new territory. Part of this is due to the overscaled cedar siding that forms a two-part system, combining a "V"-groove section with drop siding to create a big module. Offsetting the natural grain and color of the cedar siding are puce green panels of medium-density fiberboard with wood battens covering the seams.

The moment where the project diverges from the vernacular into the modern lies in the steel detailing. At the canopy on the front of the building and the ones on each end, tube steel brackets are spliced and welded to semi-circular steel plates set in the wood siding. The brackets hold aloft another tube steel beam that cantilevers beyond the edge of the roof, adding a sense of buoyancy to the assembly. This lightness continues in the detailing of the porch along the south where pairs of wide flange columns take the place of a single column member, allowing a decrease in the structure's size. Horizontal and diagonal tube steel bracing and an open wood lattice lace the columns together visually and structurally. The layering of materials and structure from solid to transparent, modulates the change in scale between the manmade and the natural and blurs the distinction between inside and out drawing people into the real classroom: the park.

Yaquina Head
Interpretive Center

Newport, Oregon 1997

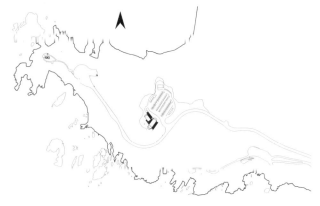

An ancient lava flow hit cold ocean water forming   143
Yaquina Head on the Oregon Coast. Today it is home
to a 126-year-old lighthouse and is a prime vantage-
point for viewing migrating gray whales. Originally
designed to crest a cliff above the beach, the interpretive center was relocated—in response to local residents' objections and with construction documents
75 percent complete—to a reclaimed rock quarry on
the 100-acre preserve. With limited funds and time
available for redesign, the 18,000-square-foot building bears a few puzzling remnants intended for its
original location. Windows meant to draw visitors outside onto a grand porch with Pacific views now face a
100-foot-tall basalt cliff.

While Miller/Hull rues the change in site, their design
for Yaquina Head proves resilient—thanks, in part, to
its straightforward scheme. Two rectangular concrete
volumes—one containing the exhibition space and the
other administrative functions—sit at a slight angle to
each other. In the space between, the lobby opens

BELOW: EARLY SKETCH

RIGHT: LOBBY OPENS TO A DOUBLE-HEIGHT PORCH
ON THE NORTH.

FAR RIGHT: PORCH, HEAVY-TIMBER FRAMING, AND
GLASS WINDOW WALL FORM AN OVERHEAD SKYLIGHT.

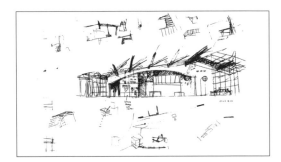

144 from the main entrance onto a double-height porch
leading to the trailhead. Its heavy-timber framing and
glass window wall turn to form a skylight overhead.

Visitors feel as if they still have one foot in the great
outdoors owing to the lobby's exposed aggregate floors
and poured-in-place concrete walls. To play up the
plastic qualities of concrete, there are oversized cuts
for openings into a gift shop and a small auditorium.
Two fourteen-foot-tall Douglas fir doors banded with
thick gusset plates roll back from the auditorium's corner entrance. A full-scale replica of the lighthouse's
lantern signals the location of the interpretive
exhibits, which were designed by Aldrich Pears
Associates, of Vancouver, British Columbia. In contrast to the articulated structure of the lobby, the
6,000-square-foot black box is an abstract and the-
atrically lit space. The life-size mural of a gray whale
and her calf that covers a curved back wall is lit with
flickering lighting to add depth. Outdoor exhibits
include universally accessible man-made tidal pools.

LEFT: SHELTERED BENCH AT THE TRAILHEAD

BELOW: CONCRETE WALLS, LOW SLUNG ROOFS, AND
CLIPPED DETAILING FIT THE STORMY OCEAN SITE.

Carved from the quarry, these pools teem with sea stars, anemones, and crabs.

Outside, thirty-foot tall concrete walls define the two main volumes and form a parapet along their length. The roof slopes toward the short end of each box where it intersects the concrete wall in an exaggerated notch. The heavy-timber roof slides through this opening, creating porches at the beginning and end of the trail. At the rear of the building this provides a sheltered resting spot tucked between steel channel brackets. At the front of the project, however, a large porch occurs over the entry to the restrooms located just to the left of the more unassuming main entrance. A covered walkway that was to extend out from the main entry to the curb—and would have resolved any confusion—was cut after the change in site required more expensive foundations.

Miller/Hull, in manipulating the scale, imbued a modest project with a strong visual presence. Oversized two-by-six-inch battens give the vertical wood siding a large-grain texture against the heavy-timber and concrete construction. Exaggerated roof scuppers jutting overhead are a dynamic counterpoint to the taut raised-seam metal roof and cropped roof rafters. A continuous vertical reveal at each corner provides articulation and prevents the large concrete volumes from appearing staid. The rugged architectural expression has a batten-down-the-hatches quality befitting the stormy ocean site.

147

LEFT: BLACK-BOX EXHIBIT SPACE

BELOW: ADMINISTRATIVE OFFICES FOR THE 100-ACRE
PRESERVE

RIGHT: TWO FOURTEEN-FOOT-TALL DOORS ROLL BACK
FROM THE AUDITORIUM'S CORNER ENTRANCE.

BELOW: EAST ELEVATION

RIGHT: A LOW VAULT CONNECTS THE TWO PARTS OF
THE HOUSE TO CREATE A TRANSPARENT SPACE.

Hansman Residence

Seattle, Washington 1997

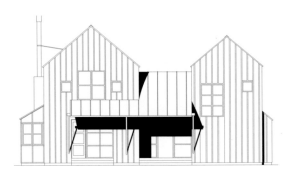

On a steep hillside overlooking Seattle, this Tuscan yellow and barn-red house evokes the proportions of its 1920s Shingle-style neighbors but is modern in the detailing. The client initially contacted Miller/Hull about adding a second floor to a one-story ranch-style house, but soon realized it was easier, and more economical, to raze the house and begin anew. The existing basement retaining walls provide the foundation for the new design. Miller/Hull split the 3,000-square-foot project into two gables with the narrow ends facing the street, continuing the rhythm of the neighborhood. A vault of metal roof connects the volumes and covers this transparent space in-between. Through windows on either side of the front door, guests can see through the house to the ferries on Elliott Bay and the Olympic Mountains beyond.

Inside, the roof starts low over the entry and curves to an eighteen-foot-high window wall, which opens onto a deck with a wide flight of steps down to the garden. The deck's steel cable railing disappears against the panoramic view. A wood and glass garage door rolls up to turn this double-height foyer and dining space into an exterior room. A system of counterweighted torsion springs makes the heavy double-glazed door feather-weight to lift. Over the dining table a chandelier six feet in diameter, made of a welded band-saw blade, salmon cans, and paper Sno-Cone cups over the bulbs by local artist Buster Simpson, also raises and lowers by counterweights. The reversed board-and-batten siding of the house's exterior wraps inside this space, and the punched windows from the second bedrooms reinforce the sense of being outside. Slicing the air overhead is a minimal steel cable and wood catwalk connecting the bedrooms and providing the spot for the most dramatic water view.

The main floor is open in plan yet the areas for the living, dining, and the kitchen are distinct. Glass doors off the entry open to a den, which connects to a covered porch onto the front yard. As the largest level area on the 60-by-120-foot lot this is the main outdoor

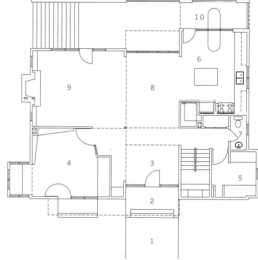

1 **WALK** 2 **PORCH** 3 **ENTRY** 4 **DEN** 5 **LAUNDRY**
6 **KITCHEN** 7 **BATH** 8 **DINING** 9 **LIVING** 10 **PORCH**

play area for the client's two young boys. Upstairs the master bedroom and bathroom are under one gable roof with the children's rooms and another bath under the other. A daylight basement contains a guestroom, storage, and large family room, with a deck opening to a flower garden capping a garage off the alley below. The vantage looking back up at the house from this alley embodies the layered quality of Seattle's hillside neighborhoods.

Throughout the house are the inventive details that make Miller/Hull's designs eminently livable. At the front door is a low built-in bench to sit, change, and stash rain boots. Its tongue-like shape repeats in a two-legged table in the kitchen that straddles the exterior wall. A tabletop double-hung window forms a pass-through to the outside grill. Built-in fir bookshelves in the living room, den, and along the stairway minimize furniture and contribute to the spaciousness of the compact house. Miller/Hull salvaged the large firebox from the old house, updating it with a rolled

steel surround studded by a grid of galvanized bolts to create the minimal fireplace that is the focal point of the living room.

On the exterior, the wood cladding reverses standard board-and-batten siding with wide twelve-inch battens over narrow one-inch boards. The battens stop four inches short around windows and through their absence mimic traditional trim board. Inverting typical construction sequencing, Miller/Hull set the windows after the installation of the siding for a precise fit between battens. At the gable ends the thin rake has the straightforward detailing of an old barn but by a twist on contemporary construction gains the articulation of its older residential neighbors. In place of roof rafters, the flat roof planks extend out to the edge of the roof, lending the underside a subtle texture. Miller/Hull's detailing is modern in its emphasis on the thin and the taut but not at the expense of texture and depth.

LEFT: ROLL-UP DOOR OPENS DINING ROOM TO AN
EXTERIOR DECK AND THE PUGET SOUND BEYOND.

BELOW: KITCHEN TABLE, LEFT, CONTINUES THROUGH
THE WINDOW TO THE OUTDOORS.

LEFT: WINDWARD SIDE OF HOUSE, A SERIES OF
CONCRETE-BLOCK WALLS NESTLED AMONG BOULDERS

BELOW: AXONOMETRIC SHOWS A CONCRETE BLOCK
SHELL INFILLED WITH TIMBER AND STEEL FRAMING.

OVERLEAF: THE HOUSE SITS ON AN ESCARPMENT
1,800 FEET ABOVE THE NACHES RIVER VALLEY.

Campbell Orchard Residence

Tieton, Washington 1998

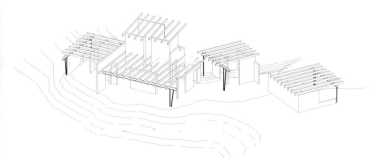

Among basalt boulders and under a century old Ponderosa pine, this house sits on an escarpment separating a lush agricultural plateau and the semi-arid Naches River Valley. Extremes in temperature and scouring winds mark the landscape. Third-generation owners of this 180-acre ranch and apple orchard, the client remembers playing as a boy along the edges of the orchard, one of several his family owned in the valley. Now a California resident, the client uses the Miller/Hull-designed residence as a base for regular visits to the Pacific Northwest.

A gravel road follows a poplar tree windbreak bordering the orchard and leads up to the new 1,350-square-feet house, which lies between two rocky ridges. The windward side of the house is a series of concrete-block retaining walls nestled into the hillside and opens to the valley 1,800 feet below. Varying in height, these walls form a loose assemblage of three interlocking "L"s that adjust to the topography. Along the orchard side, the walls parallel the orthogonal rows of trees, but at the majestic pine the wall pivots open to follow the angle of the hillside. Wood siding and glass form the remaining enclosure emphasizing the contrast between heaviness and lightness, horizontal and vertical, and inside and outside that run throughout the project.

Entry is through a stockade-like Alaskan yellow cedar door in an inscrutable concrete-block wall. It slides aside on a barn door track to reveal a private courtyard protected from the wind but open to the panoramic view. The patio wraps the east side of the house along the irregular edge of the plateau and terminates in a terrace off the master bedroom. Dark gray basalt boulders set at the edge of the polished concrete patio blur the distinction between the natural and manmade. Overhead, recycled fir timbers extend from the inside of the house to an exterior steel beam supported by a pair of steel pipe columns that frame the view. For rigidity, one leg cants outward mimicking the props holding up branches laden with apples. Galvanized

LEFT: A DOOR SLIDES ASIDE TO REVEAL A PRIVATE
AND WIND-PROTECTED COURTYARD.

BELOW: WALL SECTION AT RETAINED EARTH

RIGHT: CANTED STEEL COLUMNS

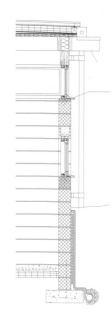

metal roofing, recalling local agricultural buildings,
covers a portion of the porch and wood rafters continue as a trellis, layering the transition from inside to
outside.

The foyer is in a knuckle between a small office and
the main house. Its horizontal wood boards are lag
bolted through a wood stud wall with exposed galvanized fasteners, giving the house a low-tech rusticity.
Inside, floor-to-ceiling windows slice the corner of
every room to open up the interior. In the office, a long
clerestory window further undercuts this boundary by
floating the timber roof above the concrete-block
walls. Two small square windows punch through the
wall to frame views of the orchard or the grassy hilltop.
The living, dining, and kitchen areas share a single
space in the main volume of the house. A ten-by-nine-
foot glass door slides into a concealed pocket opening
the corner of the living area to the patio. Lining the
back wall is a compact bath and utility area screened
by an open stair up to the loft. This guestroom pops up

LEFT: RECYCLED TIMBERS AND EXPOSED CONCRETE
IN THE LIVING/DINING ROOM

BELOW: STAINED WOOD PANELS PROVIDE ACCENTS
OF COLOR AND TEXTURE ON THE EXTERIOR.

RIGHT: FIRST FLOOR PLAN

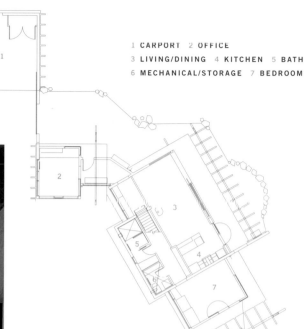

1 CARPORT 2 OFFICE
3 LIVING/DINING 4 KITCHEN 5 BATH
6 MECHANICAL/STORAGE 7 BEDROOM

above the concrete retaining wall for views out over **163**
the treetops. On the southern end of the house, the
master bedroom's full-height corner windows open the
room to a panorama of the valley.

This house marks a change in direction from other
Miller/Hull designs in its relationship to the ground.
Where other projects appear to float over the site on a
minimal slab, this one digs in and pulls the exposed
block foundation wall all the way up to the ceiling.
Insulation embedded in the interior cells of the U-
shaped concrete block allows the exposure of both
faces. On one side the wall retains the hillside and on
the other it provides bearing for the roof rafters.
Concrete block and glass are the primary enclosure
materials, with a few wood panels—stained the same
ochre and puce as the lichens on the rocks—as
accents of color and texture. The house's abstract,
graphic quality combines with a finely tuned relationship to the topography in homage to the raw landscape.

BELOW: SITE PLAN

RIGHT: THE DESIGN REFERENCES JAPANESE ARCHITECTURE
AND THE ISLAND'S VERNACULAR FARM BUILDINGS.

Ching Cabin

Maury Island, Washington 1998

164 Maury Island moors to its larger neighbor, Vashon Island, by a small spit of land in south Puget Sound. Only a fifteen-minute ferry ride from Seattle, the semi-rural island attracts both full-time residents as well as weekenders seeking a refuge from the city. This cabin for a young family of four sits along the eastern edge of a clearing on ten acres of rolling woods with trails, a small fruit orchard, and a pond. Future plans include a freestanding master bedroom suite and studio/garage connected by an arbor along the northeast edge of the meadow. With an overarching roof and articulated structure, Miller/Hull's design melds the client's interest in Japanese architecture with the island's vernacular farm buildings.

To stretch the diminutive project's 600-square-foot footprint along the back edge of the site, Miller/Hull developed the design as a string of interior and exterior spaces under a continuous gable roof. The first four of the cabin's seven structural bays contain an open living, dining, and sleeping space with small lofts for kids at either end. A four-foot-wide utility core—

containing the kitchen, a storage area, and small bathroom—runs along the east edge of the room. On the western exposure, glass tripartite doors fill the two center bays; they fold out of the way to convert the main living area into an outdoor room. Further extending the space is a wood deck cantilevered four feet out from the foundation, creating a covered porch overlooking the meadow and pond. In the fifth structural bay a breezeway connects the main living space to the garden shed that shares the rest of the structure.

At the entry on the north, the concrete raft foundation extends out as a step, with a rectangular inset of rough pebbles for a welcome mat. On the south end at the shed, the foundation notches in and is filled with gravel for tractor parking. Off the southern end of the cabin near the orchard, the pump house is a corrugated steel culvert warped into an elliptical volume.

Three glazed sections of roof cover the kitchen, the ridge of the breezeway, and the front porch, infusing interior spaces with light. The skylights' acrylic sheets

LEFT: THE CABIN BORDERS THE EASTERN EDGE OF A
CLEARING ON THE WOODED SITE.

BELOW: EXPANDED AXONOMETRIC

BELOW RIGHT: A STEEL CULVERT WRAPS THE PUMP HOUSE.

167

have the same profile as the corrugated metal roofing, allowing them to lap seamlessly over each other, creating a continuous roof plane and eliminating the awkward curb found around most skylights. The acrylic does not scratch or degrade and is much clearer than fiberglass panels. At the front porch the panels provide protection from the rain but also feather the transition between inside and outside.

In comparison to Miller/Hull's early retreats on Decatur Island, the detailing of the Ching cabin is more articulated and refined. Part of this may be due to the ten years of experience that separate the designs. The exterior's exposed columns, with an infill of dropped cedar siding or spaced cedar boards, recall the panelized construction and texture of Japanese folk architecture. While the wood joinery is not as elaborate, the reductive but elegant detailing of the roof structure suggests shared tectonic sensibility. The cabin's connection to place and transparency between inside and outside are qualities that link the design as firmly to Pacific Rim architecture as to Miller/Hull's past.

LEFT: TRANSLUCENT PANELS AT THE PORCH FEATHER
THE TRANSITION FROM OUTSIDE TO INSIDE.

BELOW: A NARROW UTILITY CORE RUNS ALONG ONE
EDGE OF THE SINGLE ROOM CABIN.

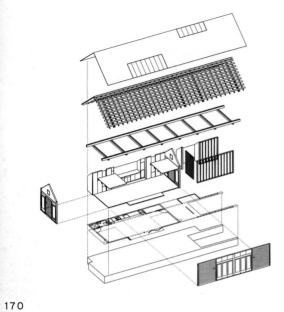

170

FAR LEFT: THE COMPACT HOUSE STANDS ON THE ONLY BUILDABLE SITE IN A WOODED RAVINE.

LEFT, TOP TO BOTTOM: WEST, NORTH, AND EAST ELEVATIONS

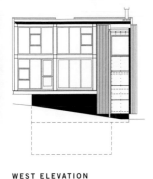

WEST ELEVATION

Michaels/Sisson Residence

Mercer Island, Washington 1998

NORTH ELEVATION

EAST ELEVATION

Where the owners of this house saw a bargain in a two-line newspaper ad—two-and-a-half acres on suburban Mercer Island for $125,000—Miller/Hull saw a challenge. The triangular site is in a wooded ravine with thick stands of maples studded with 100-foot-tall Douglas firs. A stream parallels the road and has a 25-foot setback requirement, designed to protect spawning salmon while also reducing the amount of buildable land. The clients, a young professional couple ready to start a family, also had a limited budget: $150-per-square-foot. Faced with these limitations, Miller/Hull looked to the structure for solutions as well as for architectural expression. The 2,400-square-foot house they designed sits on the only buildable spot on the site: at the base of a steep slope and on the setback line. Miller/Hull resolved two issues at once by folding a concrete block retaining wall around into a twenty-foot tall cube. The two-car garage on the lowest level set the 22-foot parameters of the square base. An intermediate concrete floor stiffens the box, making it more structurally efficient in restraining the

fifteen-foot grade change. The two-story base also lifts the house up off the floor of the dark ravine toward sunlight and views into the trees.

The main mass of the four-level house cantilevers out on steel girders over the concrete-block base to avoid damaging the root of adjacent trees. Panels of deep box-section corrugated metal float on the structural steel frame. A vertical ribbon of glass slices the private front facade and defines the narrow end of the two-story space that penetrates the two upper floors. On the back, the steel frame that will brace the house during an earthquake is infilled with glass, opening the house to the forest.

A short bridge over the stream leads to an exterior stair up to the front door. The overhang of the floor above protects it from rain. The main entry is at the first floor—containing two snug children's bedrooms and a playroom—with a generous stair continuing up to the main level of the house shared by the living, dining,

173

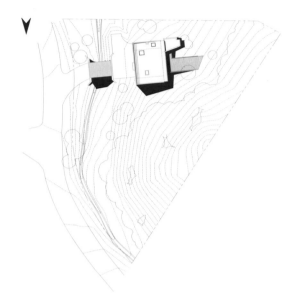

174 and the kitchen areas. It is a compact yet open space that interlocks with the second floor. A steel cable and wood decking catwalk cuts overhead across the double-height space from the front of the house to the wall of windows in back. A nine-by-ten-foot wood and glass vertical lift door glides open (thanks to counter-weighted torsion springs) encouraging the flow of the interior out onto a bridge-like deck into the ravine. The green hillside and trees enclose it, creating an intimate outdoor room.

A staircase, in a solid wedge off the back of the house, connects all the floors. Its narrow vertical strip of windows, as well as the finer wale of the corrugated siding, visually separates it from the main volume of the house. Inside, a continuous three-story bookshelf runs up one wall from the first floor entry to the underside of the ceiling at the top floor. One landing widens to suspend a trim home office between the living room

FAR LEFT: A VERTICAL WINDOW ON THE FRONT
FAÇADE HINTS AT THE TWO-STORY INTERIOR.

LEFT: WOOD WINDOWS INFILL STEEL FRAME.

and bedrooms above. A large pivot window expands **177**
the tight space out into the tree canopy and throws
light down through the open risers of the stairs. On the
fourth floor, the master bedroom and bath link to a
music room by a bridge over the living room below.
Large interlocking panels slide in varying combinations to define different degrees of privacy and to contribute to a sense of spaciousness.

The industrial palette appeals to the owners' love of
modern architecture as well as to their desire for a
low-maintenance home. The exterior corrugated metal
siding resists the Pacific Northwest's pervasive
mildew. Inside, the floor is a grid of pressed medium-
density fiberboard squares set with galvanized screws.
If stained or marred they are easy to unscrew and
replace. Overall, the exposed glue-laminated beams
and wood decking counterbalance the exposed concrete block and steel, creating a spare but warm
design. In their details, the materials also emphasize
the layered transparency of the house. The narrow

LEFT: A WOOD-AND-GLASS LIFT DOOR OPENS THE
LIVING ROOM TO THE DECK.

BELOW: EXPANDED AXONOMETRIC

RIGHT: UPSTAIRS, SLIDING PANELS ALLOW A VARIETY
OF SPATIAL CONFIGURATIONS.

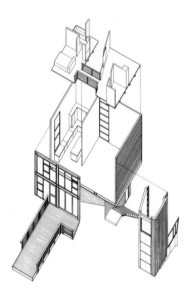

frame around the edges of the corrugated metal siding
and the notch as the panels meet at corners underscore the sense that they are planes hung on a structural frame. Stitching the panels together are windows
with mullions so thin they dissolve for an uninterrupted connection to the trees outside. Through transparency, the design appropriates the forest as a major
material in a minimal palette.

Roddy/Bale Residence

Bellevue, Washington 1998

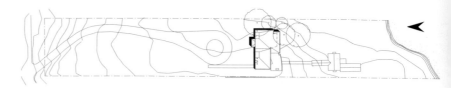

180 Before floating bridges across Lake Washington spread suburban sprawl from Seattle, Bellevue was a quiet country escape from the city. One memento of the not-so-distant past is a small fishing cottage on bass-filled Phantom Lake. For years the owners spent most of their time in this two-room cabin retreating to the main house—a 1950s ranch-style house located 200 feet from the lake—to sleep. But when the young family began to grow, they asked Miller/Hull to design a modern house that embraces the outdoors. Miller/Hull responded with a design for a metal and glass house that is compact yet transparent.

The 2,800-square-foot project stands on the spot previously occupied by the old house. The little fishing cottage remains at the water's edge as a guesthouse. The new house is a slender bar that straddles the long narrow site, dividing it into two distinct outdoor rooms. The north side features a tranquil progression from the street through the woods and across a wide lawn to the house; the back yard opens to the lake.

Two large openings link the outdoor rooms. One begins with a two-story tall window on the front facade and ends in an oversized double-height bay window on the back. A second notch carved underneath the upper floor of the house at the entry allows a direct connection between the front and back yards. This outdoor room is enclosed by glass and aluminum industrial garage doors mounted sideways to slide out of the way on an overhead barn-door track.With its polished concrete counter and deep stainless steel sink, this space is a staging area for gardening, camping trips, and outdoor entertaining.

To reach the front door, guests pass under an exposed glue-laminated beam propped up by a slender steel pipe column. The first floor is an open plan with the living room, dining, and kitchen defined by a few architectural elements. A freestanding cabinet partially screens the kitchen from the entry while housing the stove and refrigerator. The upper kitchen cabinets are boxes set at varying heights within a storefront window system. The back of each cabinet is a frosted glass window while the doors have a small clear glass panel that allows a peek inside.

The second floor bridges over a portion of the living area, creating double-height spaces on either side that

LEFT: THE STANDING-SEAM METAL SKIN HAS A
METALLIC COATING THAT SHIFTS IN COLOR.

OVERLEAF: AN OUTDOOR ROOM, ENCLOSED BY GARAGE
DOORS, CONNECTS THE FRONT AND BACK YARDS.

RIGHT: GROUND AND UPPER LEVEL PLANS

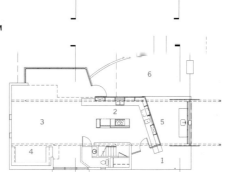

UPPER LEVEL

GROUND LEVEL

1 **ENTRY** 2 **KITCHEN** 3 **LIVING/DINING** 4 **LIBRARY**
5 **OUTDOOR ROOM** 6 **PATIO** 7 **BATH** 8 **MASTER BEDROOM**
9 **FAMILY** 10 **BEDROOM** 11 **DEN/GUEST** 12 **UTILITY**

open to the family room above. This airy multi-purpose space has views down into the living room as well as out the two-story-high windows and connects the master bedroom to an area containing a child's bedroom, a bathroom, and a small den. The child's bedroom protrudes into the large bay on the back of the house and has a floor to ceiling window with an operable panel to encourage natural ventilation. In the master bedroom the bed fits snugly in a bay window angled toward a view of the lake framed by two 100-foot cedars. The window that pops up above the roofline on the front of the house folds down overhead into a skylight that opens up the master bathroom to the sky and the towering cedars.

The exposed structure is a low-tech mix of wood framing, glue-laminated beams, and steel columns painted maroon. Two glue-laminated beams run the length of the house on either side of the first floor. Supporting them are irregularly spaced pipe columns that fall in unlikely places—like through the kitchen countertop. One column lands at the bottom of the staircase in place of a traditional newel post. On the first floor the

drywall ceiling stops a foot away from the walls, exposing the ends of the wood joists above. This makes the ceiling appear to float while providing spaces between joists for off-the-shelf galvanized steel spotlights.

Miller/Hull uses color sparingly throughout the house. The back wall of the living room is a silky cinnamon and folds around to define a small library nook with built in maple shelves. Automotive paint finishes the stair's perforated metal panel balusters and railings to achieve a pinky-copper color with flecks of silver. On the exterior, the standing-seam metal skin has a metallic coating that shifts in color from an olive green to a tawny rose depending on the brightness of the sky. Precisely punched between seams is a smattering of tiny square windows that combine with the large opening cut through the house to underscore the lightness of the taut metal skin. On the front of the house, a long narrow window pokes up above the roofline to break the box. Variety and richness come with a few restrained gestures.

183

LEFT: THE DRYWALL CEILING STOPS A FOOT AWAY
FROM THE WALLS CREATING A PLACE FOR LIGHTS.

RIGHT: OPERABLE PANELS SET WITH THE TWO-STORY
WINDOW WALL

LEFT: THE DESIGN REFERENCES EARLY-TWENTIETH-
CENTURY COMMERCIAL BUILDINGS ALONG THE STREET.

BELOW: NORTH ELEVATION

Fremont Public Association

Seattle, Washington 1998

At the Fremont Public Association (FPA) community resource center, families pick up groceries at a food bank and learn how to prepare nutritious meals in a demonstration kitchen; elderly immigrants practice English and learn citizenship skills under the same roof. Consolidating community services and volunteers previously scattered around the city allows the non-profit agency to connect key programs and better serve the disadvantaged. The 30,000-square-foot project also houses a neighborhood branch library in a prominent corner storefront space. By reinterpreting the early twentieth-century two- and three-story commercial buildings lining Wallingford's main street, Miller/Hull created a distinguished yet approachable community building.

In response to the tight budget and site constraints, the project is a compact three-story volume. A central portion of facade peels away to reveal a transparent zone through the building. On the first floor this space is an interior street, with roll-up glass and aluminum

189

LEFT: TWO-STORY ATRIUM CONNECTS THE SECOND
AND THIRD FLOORS.

BELOW: FIRST FLOOR PLAN

RIGHT: CEMENT-BOARD CLADDING EXPOSES THE
STEEL STRUCTURE AT THE MAIN ENTRY.

1 **PUBLIC GALLERY** 2 **LIBRARY** 3 **LIVING ROOM**
4 **CHECK-IN** 5 **CHILDREN'S AREA** 6 **FOOD BANK STORAGE**
7 **FOOD BANK DISTRIBUTION** 8 **KITCHEN**
9 **CONFERENCE ROOM** 10 **RESTROOM** 11 **OFFICE**

garage doors that open into a community room, a
kitchen, and the food bank. People select their own
groceries from a layout reminiscent of Seattle's
famous open-air farmer's market downtown instead of
being handed a prepackaged bag. The interior street is
also an art gallery, with tile murals and metal sculp-
tures by local artists. At the front of the building, the
family resource center and a play space for children
share the west end of the storefront facade. Since the
project's footprint fills the entire 10,000-square-foot
site, the FPA leases space behind the building for
parking, and there is an eighteen-car garage in the
basement. Subsidized bus passes and shower facilities for bicyclists encourage alternative means of com-
muting.

Upstairs, a two-story atrium visually connects the second and third floors under a long central skylight.
There is an uninterrupted view from the window wall at
the front of the building to the one at the back in this
open central space. On the third floor the exterior wall

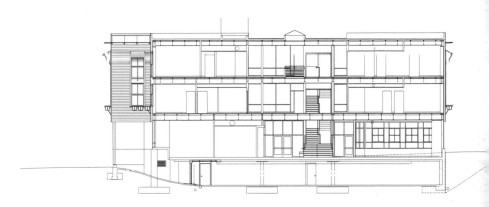

steps in along this zone, creating a covered outdoor deck for alfresco lunches. Inside, exposed steel columns differentiate the open area by peeling back layers of finishes enclosing the rest of the floor. Throughout the building the ceiling is clear-stained wood decking on top of steel bar joists painted black. Miller/Hull transfigured the modest two- and three-story commercial buildings that dot Seattle's urban neighborhoods. The design follows the same pattern of a glass storefront at street level with wood siding or brick punctuated by windows at the floors above. By peeling back the exterior siding to reveal the large steel moment frames at the openings in the front and back of the building, Miller/Hull gained structural expressiveness within a familiar building type. Where the horizontal cement-board cladding stops short to expose the structure, its edge detailing suggests a few

inches of depth—contributing to the perception of it as a skin over a steel skeleton. The vertical pairing of oversized double-hung windows avoids the numbing punched rhythm of smaller separate windows on the upper floors. At the main entry, a crimson stair tower sits behind the steel frame but in front of the curtain wall. The layers of the facade peel away as an open invitation to the community.

193

Vashon Island
Transfer and Recycling Station

Vashon Island, Washington 1999

194

Vashon Island is a semi-suburban community of farmers, artists, and families only a fifteen-minute ferry
ride from Seattle. When its old landfill reached capacity, a new one was built to accept solid waste and recy-
clables for transfer to the mainland. Miller/Hull's project is a model of sustainable design and construction,
maximizing resource efficiency and minimizing environmental impact.

The site's circulation pattern separates people and
trucks, non-paying and paying customers, and incoming and outgoing materials. An articulated metal
canopy on the front of the 8,500-square-foot building
slopes up and out, directing the public to a long wall
of openings to deposit recycling. Arriving trucks stop
first at a small weigh-station then continue to the left
along a road that slopes down and around to the back
of the building. Under a metal shed roof, truck docks
back up to the waste pit six feet below. From the pit,
materials move to the left into a shed on the south end
of the building containing a compactor that reduces
the number of trips of waste and recycling off island.

LEFT: TRUCKS STOP AT A WEIGH-STATION BEFORE
PROCEEDING TO THE RECYCLING PIT.

RIGHT, TOP TO BOTTOM, WEST AND EAST ELEVATIONS,
CROSS SECTION

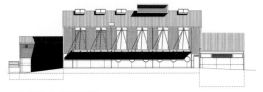

WEST ELEVATION

EAST ELEVATION

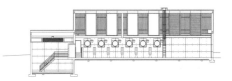

CROSS SECTION

On the opposite side of the waste pit, another shed roof covers a staff breakroom and toilets on the north end of the building.

The design is a study in volumes mediating between the scale of people on one side and large machines and trucks on the other. King County was willing to go beyond the Butler buildings typically used as long as it did not cost more. Miller/Hull accomplished this by subtly manipulating the form and materials. The project's complex sectional relationships accommodate the varying heights of cars and trucks while facilitating natural ventilation and the penetration of daylight into the interior. Large translucent panels between the lower shed roof over the truck dock and the main roof over the pit continue a few inches above the roof to break the cornice line before folding over into skylights.

The detailing emphasizes the tautness of the skin over an exposed structural steel frame, while creating texture and visual interest by juxtaposing narrow and wide corrugations of metal siding. Where crisply cut

windows and vents puncture the metal skin a knife-edge of metal trim frames the opening. The materials used throughout the project—including the steel beams and columns, metal studs and siding, insulation, gypsum wallboard, paint, and ceramic tiles—are ones with recycled content.

In a celebration of recycling, a filigree of local flora and fauna by artist Deborah Mersky surrounds the six large portholes of the public recycling bins. The installation's funding comes from King County's one-percent-for-arts program, which dedicates a portion of municipal construction budgets to architecturally integrated public art. The tracery of images from the local environment—kelp crab, starfish, anemone, black-tailed deer, and raccoon—looks delicate but is durable aluminum, cut by computer-driven water jets. Porcelain enamel on steel panels, also by Mersky, brightens the weigh-station booth. The art adds another layer in Miller/Hull's transformation of an overlooked utilitarian building type—one that forms a backdrop for community life.

197

BELOW: NORTH ELEVATION

RIGHT: WATER-JET-CUT STEEL FILIGREE SURROUNDS
THE PORTHOLES IN THE PUBLIC RECYCLING BINS.

King County Library Service Center

Issaquah, Washington 2000

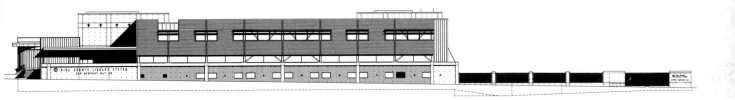

With this administrative center for the King County public library system, Miller/Hull tackled the difficult issues of building on the ragged edge of suburbia. Until recently a semi-rural area with clear lakes and stands of pine trees, Issaquah is being subsumed by sprawl as Seattle's population inches outward into the Cascade foothills. The project's site sits amidst office parks and mega-stores on a busy arterial road. To the west, across the highway, is a steep forested hillside. Protected wetlands border the property's north and east boundaries.

Miller/Hull established the project's public presence among big-box commercial buildings through astute siting and the transparency of the building's skin. They placed the majority of parking in back of the building, allowing the western facade to act as a billboard along the road. At one point Miller/Hull considered silk-screening a super-graphic of dictionary text onto the metal siding, but board members preferred the color red to recall the brick of local municipal

buildings. A ribbon window that floats it above a concrete plinth underscores the planar qualities of this elevation. Steel columns and bracing are visible through openings sliced in the skin, giving the appearance of being hung on the structural frame. Clear glass windows (unlike the ubiquitous tinted or reflective coatings generally found in office parks) are possible due to triple-tiered brise-soleil of steel channels and perforated corrugated metal.

At 80,000 square feet the Issaquah Library Service Center is the firm's largest project to date and the most programmatically complex. Early in the morning books arrive from sixty outlying branch libraries for processing, before redistribution the same day. In addition to facilitating this intricate work flow pattern, the project houses the administrative and technology departments for the library system, as well as a traveling library and public meeting rooms. The three-story building is organized vertically, with book storage and processing on the ground floor, administration and

LEFT: CORRUGATED METAL SIDING EXTENDS BEYOND
CORNERS TO APPEAR LIGHTLY LAYERED.

RIGHT: LOBBY CONNECTS SEPARATE PUBLIC AND
STAFF ENTRIES.

public meeting spaces on the second floor, and
departmental offices on the third. The site slopes
down from a ground floor public entry on the north to
a lower level loading dock on the south. The building
is a series of articulated volumes that suggest a variety of interior spaces.

Two 48-foot-square concrete cores at the north and
south ends provide structural bearing walls and wind
shear resistance. Their poured-in-place concrete walls
rise up above the rooflines to bookend the composition
and conceal rooftop mechanical equipment. Inside the
cores are program elements that require visual or
acoustical privacy such as conference rooms, private
offices, and toilets. This allows the 35-foot-wide steel-
frame bays on either side of the cores to remain open
office space. On the north, the concrete walls form a
backdrop for a curved one-story volume clad in vertical standing-seam metal siding. Currently a staging
area for a traveling library, this space may house a
branch library in the future. On the south end of the

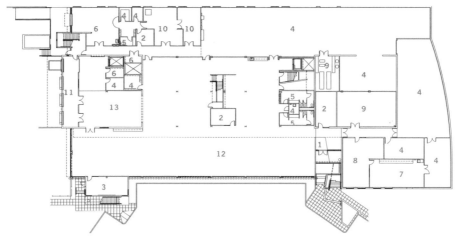

1 **LOBBY** 2 **OFFICE** 3 **CONFERENCE ROOM** 4 **STORAGE**
5 **RESTROOM** 6 **MECHANICAL/EQUIPMENT** 7 **PRINTING**
8 **GRAPHICS** 9 **EVALUATION** 10 **SHOP** 11 **LOAD/UNLOAD**
12 **CATALOGING & PROCESSING** 13 **SHIPPING**

building, the core protrudes just beyond the main mass of the building at the loading dock. A fine web of steel rods angles down the three-story end wall to pick up the edge of a canopy that protects the trucks unloading books.

The main public entry is off a raised plaza, through a series of light steel frames that balance a long narrow canopy overhead. From this point visitors are directed to the offices or through a two-story lobby into public meeting rooms. The lobby is a minimal space inside the concrete core with a perforated aluminum balcony projecting into it at the second floor. A skylight washes one wall with natural light. This end of the building can be secured separately for public meetings in the evenings.

Staff enters the lobby area by a stairway from a parking lot on the east side of the building. Inside, two generous stairs tie the three levels of the workspaces together. In the open office space clouds of suspend-

ed ceiling reflect daylight into the interior and control sound while revealing the open-web steel joists and metal decking along the exterior wall. Through a fine layer of steel columns and diagonal bracing the vertical wall of trees across the road appears through the expanse of windows as a swath of lush green.

To underscore the sense that the metal clad exterior walls are lightly layered over the structure, the corrugated siding does not wrap around corners but extends out beyond some nine inches. A blue steel column is the next layer back and the window frames are set back within it. The elegant corner detailing realizes the design's larger promise of floating planes. It is in this astute handling of small and large scales that the building offers ways to extend into the public realm the modern tradition readily found in the region's residential architecture.

BELOW: WEST ELEVATION

RIGHT: THE DESIGN RECALLS THE FORMS OF THE
ISLAND'S EARLY BARNS AND SAWMILLS.

Bainbridge Island City Hall

Bainbridge Island, Washington 2000

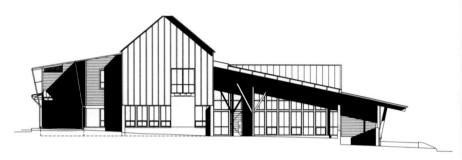

206 In the early 1900s, Bainbridge Island was home to Port Blakely, the largest timber mill in the world—churning out 500,000 board feet of lumber a day. Ironically, the new City Hall for this once deforested island now boasts one of the largest installations of certified wood from forests with stringent stewardship practices. One of ten Earth Day 2000 projects recognized for sustainable design by the American Institute for Architects, the City Hall also exemplifies Miller/Hull's subtle redefinition of a non-existent Pacific Northwest urbanism. With the astute placement of a few simple volumes a new civic center thrives in what was previously an amorphous parking lot.

The project is just off the main street through Winslow—the disembarking point for the 35-minute ferry crossing from Seattle. To ease the 24,000-square-foot City Hall into a row of low-scale retail and residential projects, Miller/Hull placed one gable end of the long, narrow volume along Madison Avenue and removed the majority of the parking to behind the building. By pushing the project to the north west corner of the five-acre site, Miller/Hull provided a clearing for a new town square bounded by the City Hall, the existing Performing Arts Center, and in the near future a mixed-use project. On the civic center's concrete plaza a minimal steel structure supports loud speakers during public gatherings, awnings over a popular weekend farmer's market, and banners during outdoor performances on summer evenings.

The new City Hall consolidates previously scattered departments in a straightforward design that recalls the additive forms of the island's earlier barns and sawmills. To break down the mass of the project, Miller/Hull looked to the way vernacular roofs extend out—but not always at the same slope—over side aisles to enclose more space. On the north side of the main two-story gabled volume, a narrow two-story extension continues the roof at a flatter slope. Along the south side, a continuous strip of skylight separates a wide plane of roof down to a low porch covering a

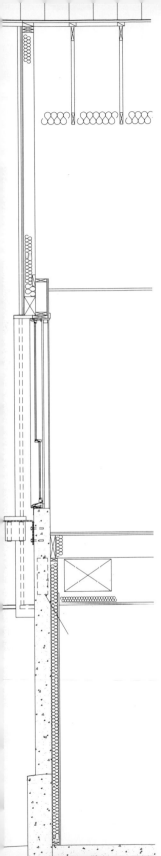

FAR LEFT: EXTERIOR MATERIALS CONTINUE INSIDE
ALONG A DOUBLE-HEIGHT INTERIOR STREET.

LEFT: SECTION THROUGH WEST WALL

OVERLEAF LEFT: CITY COUNCIL CHAMBERS

OVERLEAF RIGHT: TILES IN COUNTERTOPS ARE PART
OF PUBLIC ART INSTALLATIONS.

walkway. The roof slopes up at a valley on the east end of the building to signal the location of the council chambers and visually terminate the long elevation.

A double-height porch on Madison Avenue leads into a glazed lobby with a large-scale steel map of the island visible from the street—one of several public art works incorporated into the project. An interior street connects this entry to one off the new civic plaza and provides the organizing element for the design. The exterior board-and-batten siding cladding wraps inside; windows from offices on the second floor open onto it and continue the illusion of being outside. A skylight physically separates the main volume from the shed over the hall and is knit back together by glue-laminated rafters. Branches from a row of wood columns reach up to brace the rafters and also bring the scale of the two-story space down to an intimate level at the counters that run along both sides of the hall. The clear layout—on the north is the planning department and on the south is public works—simplifies trips to city hall by providing one-stop services for citizens; it is possible to get a marriage license and a building permit in the same place. The hubbub of every day bureaucratic functioning bubbles in the background but a semi-permeable layering of architectural elements define space for the city staff space to work uninterrupted.

A grand steel and wood-panel stair leads up to administrative and executive offices on the upper level. The mayor has a large second floor window onto Madison with a modified Pope's balcony-cum-flower box. A decorative metal gate secures the stairway and the main hall, allowing evening use of the city council chamber. A kings post truss supports the valley in the roof over the chamber and underscores the multi-directional flexibility of the room. Large windows open corners of the chamber to the porch and plaza, allowing the pubic a glimpse of democracy in action.

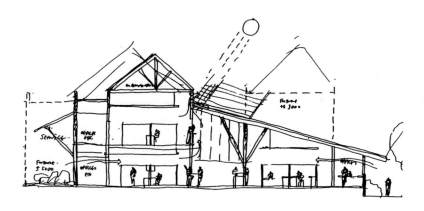

212 Miller/Hull also linked environmental with social ideals through a green agenda in the design and construction of the project. Over the years they have found success in focusing on two or three areas per project. In this case the emphasis was on certified wood, natural daylighting, and indoor air quality. Although the old ex-timber executives on the island were suspicious of wood from forests managed by a non-profit certifying agency, the project is now a showcase for this new direction in green buildings. The skylight running down the center of the building and the narrow open plan guarantee that no desk is more than twenty feet from daylight. For healthier indoor air, openings above the windows in the main hall enhance air circulation and low volatile organic compounds and non-toxic finishes are used throughout the building.

The design tweaks the simple volumes and taut skins of the island's barns and timber mills. The size of the boards and battens cladding the exterior are slightly larger than normal to play with the scale of the building. In some sections, the siding peels back, revealing the concrete base or the wood-frame structure to emphasize the planar nature of the building skin. Openings cut in the main volume center on the structure to reveal a wood post with windows on either side, underscoring the sense of layers. Miller/Hull's detailing transformed the vernacular into the modern and resolved the dichotomy in public sentiment for an unostentatious City Hall that nevertheless projects a strong civic presence.

DEGREES OF SEPARATION

Miller/Hull successfully negotiates the fine line between change (which often occurs for its own sake) and continuity (which often devolves into dull repetition). Change is evident in their emblematic details: the attenuated struts that hold up overhangs, circular windows punched in doors and walls, and the "V" of steel rod supports. These architectural elements appear, undergo a process of refinement over several projects, and then disappear before their visual freshness expires. At the same time, the fundamental values underlying Miller/Hull's work— the connection to the outdoors, lightness, transparency, and an economy of means—provide a malleable continuum. As the designers mature and the projects become more complex, there is a more subtle means revealed in their ideas that give meaningful context to the earlier work.

One example is Miller/Hull's iconic roofs. In their exaggeration of the simple shed forms of the region's timber mills they distill Pacific Northwest architecture to its essence: shelter from the rain. Under an overreaching roof, walls are superfluous and, in a mild climate, walls are a much less important element, primarily a barrier between the inside and the outdoors. As Miller/Hull's emphasis shifts from overscaled roofs to flat volumes, beginning with the Garfield Community Center and then with the Roddy/Bale and Michaels/Sisson residences, it becomes clear that the uninterrupted relationship between interior and exterior is their focus. Few Pacific Northwest architects explore this relationship to the degree that Miller/Hull has and it continues to distinguish their work. The glazed garage doors that whisk entire walls out of the way are still present but at the Roddy/Bale residence they combine to create a new type of space that is neither exterior nor interior but changes easily to fit its use. There are also finer variations in the way Miller/Hull penetrates the building skin. In early projects the openings tend to be one extreme or the other: punched windows in a solid wall or glass infill between exposed columns and beams. In more recent

GIRVIN CABIN SITE, DECATUR ISLAND, WASHINGTON

projects a combination of these two attitudes appears with the Lake Washington School District Resource Center and the Bainbridge Island City Hall to emphasize the layered quality of the cladding. In both designs large openings in the exterior wall center on the structural grid to reveal a column with windows on either side. But it is the metal clad volume of the Roddy/Bale residence that makes clear that Miller/Hull has less interest in tectonics than in lightness and transparency. Openings cut, slice, and punch through the house's taut skin to imbue it with the buoyancy of a tent in the woods. Over time, the graphic, two-dimensional quality of Miller/Hull's early projects is ceding to the scenographic. The vast roof over the Water Pollution Control Laboratory is less a unifying gesture than the consideration of a fifth facade visible from the St. John's suspension bridge overhead. Part of this is the result of the increasing size and programmatic complexity of the projects that are not reducible to a single image. But it is also due to the role their projects play in untangling and transforming amorphous town centers or the jumbled edges of suburbia. Instead of the singular, identifiable image of Olympic Community College's front porch beckoning along a wooded road, the Bainbridge Island City Hall projects a multi-faceted presence that reinforces the variety of public uses of a civic center. While Miller/Hull's new projects are larger and more complex, the budgets are not necessarily more generous. The lessons in economy that fostered their innovation with off-the-shelf materials still resonate as they continue to challenge the constraints of time, money, and conventional programs. This tenacity, as well as the rigor and clarity of their early work, remain but are never formulaic. Instead there is a sense of intuitiveness in the proportions of volumes, the texture and colors, and in the connection to the past that gives Miller/Hull's designs an emotional authenticity. In a region concerned with preserving its uniqueness, this accessibility to modernism is their unique contribution to a vibrant architecture of the Pacific Northwest.

215

PROJECT DATA

Notvotny Cabin
Decatur Island, WA

Building Area: 840 square feet

Site Area: 100 s.f. diameter circle

Client: Cynthia Novotny

Project Team: Bob Hull, FAIA
(design partner-in-charge)

Engineers: Greg Hiatt (structural)

General Contractor: Habitat Construction,
Pete Pederson

Completion Date: 1990

Boeing Cafeteria
Tukwila, WA

Building Area: 10,000 square feet

Client: Boeing Company/Boeing
Engineering and Construction

Project Team: Robert Hull, FAIA, (partner-in-charge, design); Norman Strong, AIA (partner-in-charge); Lisa Kirkendall, AIA, (project manager); Steve Tatge, AIA (project architect)

Engineers: KPFF Engineers
(structural/civil); D.W. Thomson
Consultants, Ltd. (mechanical); Sparling
Company (electrical)

Consultants: Bruce Dees and Associates
(landscape architects); Restaurant
Design & Sales, Redmond (kitchen
design)

General Contractor: Ferguson Construction

Completion Date: October 1991

Marquand Retreat
Naches River Valley, Washington

Building Area: 450 s.f.

Site Area: 200 Acres

Client: Ed Marquand

Project Team: David Miller, FAIA,
(partner-in-charge, design); Philip
Christophides, AIA, (project manager)

Engineers: Margorie Lund (structural)

General Contractor: Vetch & Petersen

Completion Date: November 1992

University of Washington Coaches Boat House
Seattle, WA

Building Area: 3024 s.f.

Client: University of Washington

Project Team: Robert Hull, FAIA,
(partner-in-charge)

Consultants: KCM (structural), Jongejan
Gerrard McNeal (landscape architect)

General Contractor: Hurlen Construction Co.

Completion Date: April 1993

Girvin Cabin
Decatur Island, WA

Building Area: 1,950 s.f.

Site Area: 100 ft. diameter circle

Client: Tim Girvin and Kathleen Roberts

Project Team: Robert Hull, FAIA
(partner-in-charge); Victoria Carter
(project manager)

Engineers: C.T. Engineering (structural)

General Contractor: Avery Builders

Completion date: May 1994

Garfield Community Center
Seattle, Washington

Building Area: 20,000 s.f.

Site Area: 3 acres

Client: Seattle Parks and Recreation

Project Team: Robert Hull, FAIA,
(partner-in-charge, design); Norman
Strong, AIA, (partner-in-charge); Steve
Tatge, AIA, Philip Christofides (project
managers); Amy Lelyveld, Christine
Arthur (project team)

Landscape Architect: Murase Associates

Engineers: H.K. Kim Engineers (structural);
Greenbusch Group (mechanical);
Atkinson/Reichard (electrical);
S-R Design Company (civil)

Consultants: Makers (planning);
C3MG (cost)

General Contractor: Lamb Longo

Completion Date: November 1994

Olympic College, Shelton
Shelton, WA

Building Area: 8000 s.f.

Site Area: 27-acres

Client: Olympic College

Project Team: Robert Hull, FAIA,
(partner-in-charge, design); Scott Wolf
(project manager)

Engineers: AKB Engineers (Structural),
Greenbusch Group (Mechanical),
S-R Design Group (Civil)

Landscape Architect: S-R Design Group

Consultants: C3 Management Group
(Cost Consultants)

General Contractor: Construction
Enterprises & Contractors, Inc.

Completion Date: October 1995

NW Federal Credit Union
Seattle, WA

Building Area: 40,000 square feet

Site Area: 60,980 s.f. (1.4 acres)

Client: NW Federal Credit Union

Project Team: Dave Miller, FAIA,
(partner-in-charge, design), Dian Roberts,
AIA; Scott Wolf, AIA; Aidan Stretch,
(project architects); Steve Southerland,
AIA; Holden Withington (project managers)

Engineers: H.K. Kim Engineers
(structural); S-R Design Co. (civil);
Wood/Harbringer (mechanical); Sparling
(electrical), Geo. Engineers (soil)

Consultants: Paladino Consulting
(sustainable design); Jongetan/Gerrard/
McNeal (landscape); Genette Voynow
(lighting); The Greenbusch Group
(acoustical); Mark Smith (branch bank
construction)

General Contractor: Lease Crutcher Lewis

Completion Date: January 1996

Tahoma National Cemetery
Kent, Washington

Building Area: 160 acres

Site Area: 1,230 s.f. public information
building (main entrance); four 832 s.f.
open-air committal shelters; 4,165 s.f.
office space; 9,960 s.f. maintenance/
vehicle storage; 21,825 s.f. service yard.

Client: National Cemetery System, US
Department of Veteran Affairs,
Washington, D.C.

Project Team: David Miller, FAIA,
(partner-in-charge, design); Victoria
Carter, Scott Wolf, AIA, Peter Wolff
(project architects).

Engineers: H.K. Kim Engineers (structural);
Sider & Byers Associates (mechanical);
Atkinson-Reichard (electrical)

Consultants: Jongejan Gerrard McNeal
(landscape); C3 Management Group
(estimator)

General Contractor: Aldrich & Associates

Completion Date: March, 1997

Hansman Residence
Seattle, WA

Building Area: 3000 s.f.

Site Area: 9600 s.f.

Client: John & Lori Hansman

Project Team: Bob Hull, FAIA
(design partner-in-charge);
Victoria Carter (project manager)

Consultants: Beers/Withington
(landscape architect); C.T. Engineers
(structural)

General Contractor: Hansman
Construction

Completion Date: 1997

Discovery Park Visitor Center
Seattle, Washington

Building Area: 11,500 s.f.

Site Area: 2.5 acres

Client: Seattle Parks & Recreation

Project Team: Robert Hull, FAIA
(partner-in-charge, design); Steve Tatge,
AIA (project manager), Victoria Carter
(project architect)

Engineers: H.K. Kim Engineer (structural);
The Greenbusch Group (mechanical);
Berona/Langebartel (electrical);
AKB Engineers, Inc. (Civil).

Consultants: Worthy & Associates (landscape architect); Raven Communications
(interpretive design); Kanezo Anyo
Domoto, Architect (specifications);
Bruce Meyers (artist).

General Contractor: Construction International

Completion Date: 1997

Water Pollution Control Laboratory
Portland, Oregon

Building Area: 40,000 s.f. (15,000 s.f. of laboratories + 25,000 s.f. of services)

Site Area: 7.6 acres

Client: Bureau of Environmental Services

Project Team: Robert Hull, FAIA (partner-in-charge, design); Norman Strong (partner-in-charge); Richard Whealan, AIA (project manager, design and documents); Steven Tatge, AIA (project manager, planning)

Engineers: KPFF Engineers (structural); Building System RX, Northwest (mechanical); Westlake Associates (civil); CH2M Hill (geotechnical); Cochran Broadway (electrical)

Consultants: SERA Architect, P.C. (architect of record); Portland Gas & Electric Commercial Efficiency Program; Charlie Brown, University of Oregon (energy efficiency); Turner Construction Company (construction managers); Anixter Brother, Inc. (voice & data); Dan Merkt (artist); CH2M Hill (lab planning); Murase Associates (landscape architect); Strode Eckert Photographic (photographer)

General Contractor: U.S. Pacific Builders

Completion Date: February 1997

Point Roberts Border Station
Point Roberts, Washington

Building Area: 12,000 s.f.

Site Area: 2 acres

Client: US Government, General Services

Administration, Department of Immigration & Naturalization United States Customs Service. Auburn, Washington

Project Team: Dave Miller, FAIA (partner-in-charge, design); Craig Curtis, AIA (partner-in-charge); Christine Arthur, Scott Wolf, AIA (project managers); Peter Wolf, Annie Han, Chris Patano (project team)

Engineers: KPFF Consulting Engineers (civil/structural); Wood/Harbinger Inc. (mechanical); Sparling (electrical); Geo Engineers (geotechnical)

Consultants: Ackroyd (cost consultants); Art Anderson & Associates (construction administration); EDAW, Inc. (landscape)

General Contractor: Arango Construction Co.

Completion Date: June 1997

Lake Washington School District Resource Center
Redmond, Washington

Building Area: 55,000 s.f.

Site Area: 1.9 acres

Client: Lake Washington School District No. 414

Project Team: Norman Strong, AIA (partner-in-charge); Robert Hull, FAIA (partner-in-charge of design); Richard Whealan (project manager); Sian Roberts, Annie Han (project architect)

Engineers: KPFF Consulting Engineers (structural/civil); The Greenbusch Group (mechanical); Sparling (electrical/communications)

Consultants: Allbee-Romein (systems furnishings); C3 Management Group (costing); Hewitt (landscape architects)

General Contractor: Crownover Construction Co.

Completion Date: August 1997

North Kitsap Transportation Center
Poulsbo, WA

Building Area: 20,000 s.f.

Site Area: 5 acres

Client: North Kitsap School District

Project Team: Norman Strong (partner-in-charge, design); Amy Lelyveld (project architect)

Engineers: S-R Design Co. (landscape); CT Engineering (structural); The Greenbusch Group (mechanical); Coffman Engineers (electrical)

Consultants: The Robinson Group (estimating)

General Contractor: Lugo Construction

Completion Date: December 1997

Yaquina Head Interpretive Center
Newport, Oregon

Building Area: 18,000 square feet

Site Area: 120 acres

Client: US Government Bureau of Land Management, Portland, Oregon

Project Team: Robert Hull, FAIA, (partner-in-charge, design); Craig Curtis, AIA, (partner-in-charge); Christine

Arthur, (project manager); Sian Roberts,
Peter Wolff, (project team)

Engineers: KCM Inc. (structural/civil);
CBG Engineers (mechanical/electrical);
Hong West Engineers (geotechnical)

Consultants: Aldrich Pears Assoc., Ltd.
(interpretive exhibitry); Murase
Associates (landscape); Rider Hunt
Ackroyd (costing); Towne, Richards,
Chaudiere (acoustics); Douglas Welch
Design Assoc., Ltd. (lighting); Stephen
Dow Beckham (interpretive research).

General Contractor: Slayden
Construction; Stayton, Oregon.

Completion Date: June 1997

Michaels/Sisson Residence
Mercer Island, Washington

Building Area: 2,400 s.f.

Site Area: 2.5 Acres

Client: Larry Sisson, Amy Michaels

Project Team: Robert Hull, FAIA,
(partner-in-charge, design);
Amy DeDominicis, (project manager)

Engineers: Dayle B. Houk (structural)

Consultants: Quantum Windows
(vertical-lift window engineering);
James F. Housel (photographer);
Art Grice (phogtographer)

General Contractor: Jeffrey Davis
Construction

Completion Date: October 1998

Ching Cabin
Maury Island, WA

Building Area: 600 s.f.

Site Area: Ten Acres

Client: Ching family

Project Team: Dave Miller, FAIA
(design partner-in-charge)

Engineers: Dayle B. Houk & Company
(structural)

General Contractor: Bellan Construction

Completion Date: 1998

Campbell Orchard Residence
Tieton, Washington

Building Area: 1,350 square feet

Site Area: 180 acre ranch

Client: Sharon and Craig Campbell

Project Team: Craig Curtis, AIA
(partner-in-charge, design), Sian Roberts
(project manager)

Engineers: Dayle B. Houk & Co. (structural)

Consultants: Sharon Campbell Interior
Design

General Contractor: VK Powell

Completion Date: March 1998

Roddy/Bale Residence
Bellevue, Washington

Building Area: 2,800 s.f.

Site Area: 45,000 s.f.

Client: Jan Roddy & Marc Bale

Project Team: Robert Hull, FAIA,

(partner-in-charge, design);
Amy Lelyveld (project manager)

Engineers: CT Engineering (structural);
S-R Design Co. (civil)

General Contractor: Jerry Fulks

Completion Date: December, 1998

Vashon Island Transfer and Recycling Station
Vashon Island, WA

Building Area: 8500 s.f. Transfer
Building; 400 s.f. scale house

Site Area: 11 acres

Client: King County Solid Waste Division

Project Team: Norm Strong (partner-in-
charge); Sian Roberts (project manager);
Laurie Fanger (project architect)

Engineers: Thomas Wright, Inc. (civil);
CH2Mhill (mechanical/electrical); H.K.
Kim Engineers, Inc. (structural); HWA
Geosciences, Inc. (testing/geotechnical)

Consultants: Susan Black and
Associates, Inc. (Landscape Architect);
Triangle Associates (Public Involvement);
Deborah Mersky (artist/educator)

General Contractor: Pease Construction
Inc., Lakewood, WA

Completion Date: March 1999

CHRONOLOGY OF BUILDINGS AND PROJECTS

1977   **Warren Residence**
        Moses Lake, Washington

1979   **Cedar Hills Activities Building**
        Maple Valley, Washington

        **Evergreen State College
        Activities Building**
        Olympia, Washington
        (unbuilt)

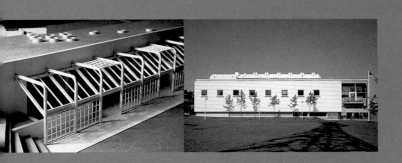

1980   **University of Washington
        Health Sciences Projects**
        Seattle, Washington

        Hansen Residence
        Moses Lake, Washington

1982   **The Kimmick Earth
        Shelter Residence**
        Cle Elum, Washington

        Alki Beach Structures
        Seattle, Washington
        (competition entry)

        **King County Courthouse
        Renovation**
        Seattle, Washington

        Mercy Earth Shelter Residence
        Lake Marcel, Washington

1984   **Central Park Structures**
        Bellevue, Washington
        (competition entry)

1985   **The AWARE Shelter**
        Juneau, Alaska

        Washington State Pavilion
        Vancouver, British Columbia
        (competition entry)

1986   **King County/Metro
        Environmental Lab**
        Seattle, Washington

1987   **Gorton/Bounds Cabin**
        Decatur Island, Washington

        **Seattle Central
        Community College Marine
        Technology Facility**
        Seattle, Washington

        Metzger Residence
        Marysville, Washington

        **Meadowdale Beach Rangers
        Residence & Park Structures**
        Lynnwood, Washington

1988   **First Hill Diagnostic (MRI)
        Imaging Center**
        Seattle, Washington

        Adams Elementary School
        Seattle, Washington

**University of Washington
Athletic Program Offices**
Seattle, Washington
(unbuilt)

1989 **Washington State University
Food Services Building**
Pullman, Washington

Bolen Cabin
Decatur Island, Washington

1990 **Evergreen State College Art
Studios Addition**
Olympia, Washington

Novotny Cabin
Decatur Island, Washington

Fadem Residence
Orcas Island, Washington

**Fisheries Teaching & Research
Facility at the University of
Washington**
Seattle, Washington

Weissbourd Residence
Bainbridge Island, WA

1991 **Boeing Cafeteria**
Tukwila, Washington

Velodrome & Bicycle Museum
Redmond, Washington
(unbuilt)

**Lake Washington United
Methodist Church**
Kirkland, Washington

**Seattle Central Community
College Wood Technology
Facility**
Seattle, Washington

**University of Washington
Henderson Hall Addition**
Seattle, Washington
(unbuilt)

Jackson Cabin
Decatur Island, Washington

Peoehman Residence
Orcas Island, Washington

1992 **Marquand Retreat**
Naches River Valley,
Washington

Snake Lake Nature Center
Tacoma, Washington

**Northaven Assisted
Living Facility**
Seattle, Washington

Lakeside School Arts Facility
Seattle, Washington
(competition entry)

**Weaver Bergh
Residence & Studio**
Bainbridge Island, Washington

1993 **University of Washington
Coaches Boathouse**
Seattle, Washington

Community Center
SeaTac, Washington

221

McCaw Cellular Offices
Kirkland, Washington

1994   Girvin Cabin
Decatur Island, Washington

Garfield Community Center
Seattle, Washington

Fire Station No. 8
Bellevue, Washington

1995   Olympic College
Shelton, Washington

Passenger-Only Ferry Terminal
Seattle, Washington
(unbuilt)

Roundy Residence
at Ebeys Landing
Coupeville, Washington

1996   NW Federal Credit Union
Seattle, Washington

McCollum Park & Ride Facility
Tacoma, Washington

Community Center
Issaquah, Washington

Camarda Residence
Vashon Island, Washington

Patagonia Worldwide
Distribution Center
Reno, Nevada

City Light Headquarters Offices
Seattle, Washington

Rolf and Hunner Residences
Electric City, Washington

1997   Lake Washington School
District Resource Center
Redmond, Washington

Tahoma National Cemetery
Kent, Washington

Point Roberts Border Station
Point Roberts, Washington

North Kitsap
Transportation Center
Poulsbo, Washington

Water Pollution Control Lab
Portland, Oregon
SERA ARCHITECTS,
PC-ARCHITECTS OF RECORD

Discovery Park Visitor Center
Seattle, Washington

Yaquina Head Interpretive Center
Newport, Oregon

Hansman Residence
Seattle, Washington

Marks Residence
Vashon Island, Washington

1998   Campbell Orchard Residence
Tieton, Washington

Ching Cabin
Maury Island, Washington

Michaels/Sisson Residence
Moroor Island, Washington

Roddy/Bale Residence
Bellevue, Washington

Fremont Public Association
Seattle, Washington

**Harborview Teaching &
Research Facility**
Seattle, Washington
CONSULTANT TO MBT ARCHITECTS

Metro Van Distribution Center
Redmond, Washington

Magnolia Community Pool
Seattle, Washington

Jones Cabin
Stuart Island, Washington

1999 **Transfer & Recycling Station**
Vashon Island, Washington

**Tillamook Forest
Interpretive Center**
Tillamook, Oregon

**Office Building 2 Improvements
at the Capitol Campus**
Olympia, Washington

Seattle Water Lab
Seattle, Washington

Dixon Residence
Grande Ronde, Washington

2000 **King County Library
Service Center**
Issaquah, Washington

Bainbridge Island City Hall
Bainbridge Island, Washington

Olympic College
Poulsbo, Washington

**Washington State University
Shock Physics Building**
Pullman, Washington

**Festival Pavilion
at Seattle Center**
Seattle, Washington

**Seattle Pacific University
Science Building Phase I**
Seattle, Washington

223

AWARDS

224

2000

Honor Award, AIA Seattle Chapter
Bainbridge Island City Hall/Bainbridge
Island, WA

Merit Award, AIA Seattle Chapter
Roddy/Bale Residence/Bellevue, WA

Honor Award, AIA Washington Civic
Design Awards
Bainbridge Island City Hall/Bainbridge
Island, WA

Earth Day Top 10 National Projects
AIA/Best Examples of
Environmentally Responsible Design
Bainbridge Island City Hall/Bainbridge
Island, WA

Honor Award, AIA National
Point Roberts Border Facility/Point
Roberts, WA

Honor Award, AIA NW & Pacific Region
Point Roberts Border Facility/Point
Roberts, WA

Honor Award, AIA NW & Pacific Region
Ching Cabin/Maury Island, WA

Merit Award, AIA NW & Pacific Region
Campbell Orchard Residence/Tieton, WA

1999

Federal Design Achievement Award
Point Roberts Border Facility/Point
Roberts, WA

Honor Award, AIA National
Olympic College Shelton/Shelton, WA

Merit Award, AIA Seattle Chapter
Ching Cabin/Maury Island, WA

Honor Award ASLA,
National Water Pollution Control
Laboratory/Portland, OR

Commendation Award, AIA Seattle
Yaquina Head Interpretive
Center/Newport, OR

Honor Award, AIA NW & Pacific Region
Michaels/Sisson Residence/Mercer
Island, WA

Merit Award, Sunset Magazine
Ching Cabin/Maury Island, WA

Citation Award, Sunset Magazine
Michaels/Sisson Residence/Mercer
Island, WA

Citation Award, Sunset Magazine
Marks Residence/Vashon Island, WA

1998

Earth Day Top 10 National Projects
AIA/Best Examples of Environmentally
Responsible Design
Patagonia Distribution Center/Reno, NV

GSA Honor Award for Design Excellence
Point Roberts Border Facility/Point
Roberts, WA

Honor Award, AIA Seattle Chapter
Point Roberts Border Facility/Point
Roberts, WA

Honor Award, AIA Seattle Chapter
Michaels/Sisson Residence/Mercer
Island, WA

Merit Award, AIA Seattle Chapter
Campbell Orchard Residence/Tieton, WA

Commendation Award, AIA Seattle Chapter
Water Pollution Control
Laboratory/Portland, OR

Citation Award, Conceptual,
AIA Seattle Chapter
Grande Ronde Residence/Grande Ronde, WA

Citation Award, American Wood Council
Discovery Park Visitor Center/Seattle, WA

Honor Award, American Wood Council
Ching Cabin/Maury Island, WA

Merit Award, AIA NW & Pacific Region
Discovery Park Visitor Center/Seattle, WA

Best of Program Award, National CMA/AIA
Campbell Orchard Residence/Tieton, WA

Best Public Building,
OCAPA & Oregon Chapter ACI
Yaquina Head Interpretive
Complex/Newport, OR

Special Mention Award,
Laboratory of the Year Program
Research & Development Magazine
Water Pollution Control
Laboratory/Portland, OR

1997
Merit Award, AIA Seattle Chapter
Discovery Park Visitor Center/Seattle, WA

Sustainable Design Award, Boston
Society of Architects
Patagonia Distribution Center/Reno, NV

Merit Award, Best Projects of the Year/1997
Construction Data News Magazine
Yaquina Head Interpretive
Complex/Newport, OR

Honor Award, AIA Portland Chapter
Water Pollution Control
Laboratory/Portland, OR

Honor Award, Interior Design Assoc.,
Portland Chapter
Water Pollution Control
Laboratory/Portland, OR

Excellence on The Waterfront
Annual Award
Water Pollution Control
Laboratory/Portland, OR

Merit Award for New Construction,
American Society of Landscape
Architects, Washington Chapter
Water Pollution Control Laboratory.
Portland/OR

Merit Award, Portland General Electric's
Energy User News
Water Pollution Control
Laboratory/Portland, OR

Safety Award for Ergonomic
Improvements, City of Portland's Risk
Management Group
Water Pollution Control
Laboratory/Portland, OR

Merit Award for Stormwater Design,
Metro of Portland
Water Pollution Control
Laboratory/Portland, OR

Merit Award, BPA Architecture + Energy
Water Pollution Control
Laboratory/Portland, OR

Extraordinary Use of Public Funds Award
AIA, ASID and IIDA Portland Chapters
Water Pollution Control
Laboratory/Portland, OR

Merit Award, AIA NW & Pacific Region
Camarda Residence/Vashon Island, WA

Honor Award, Sunset Magazine
Island House/Decatur Island, WA

Merit Award, Sunset Magazine
Camarda Residence/Vashon Island, WA

Citation Award, Sunset Magazine
Hansman Residence/Seattle, WA

1996
Commendation Award, AIA Seattle
Camarda Residence/Vashon Island, WA

Citation Award, AIA Seattle Chapter
Point Roberts Border Station/Point
Roberts, WA

Grand Award, AIA NW & Pacific Region
Olympic College Shelton/Shelton, WA

Citation Award, BPA Architecture + Energy
NW Federal Credit Union/Seattle, WA

Award of Excellence, Sunset Magazine
Camarda Residence/Vashon Island WA

Top Merit Award,
AIA/NCMA Design Awards
Marquand Retreat/Yakima, WA

Award for Excellence in Planning & Design
Record Houses Issue, April 96
Island House/Decatur Island, WA

1995
Merit Award, American Wood Council
Olympic College Shelton/Shelton, WA

Honor Award, AIA Seattle Chapter
Olympic College Shelton/Shelton, WA

Honor Award, AIA Seattle Chapter
Garfield Community Center/Seattle, WA

Merit Award, AIA NW & Pacific Region
Island House/Decatur Island, WA

Citation for Future Work,
AIA Portland Chapter
Water Pollution Control Lab/Portland, OR

Special Recognition
Masonry Institute of Washington
Garfield Community Center/Seattle, WA

Home of the Decade Award, 1980–1990
AIA/Seattle Times Home of the Month
Mercy Residence/Lake Marcel, WA

1994
Merit Award, American Wood Council
Island Cabin/Decatur Island, WA

Merit Award, AIA Seattle Chapter
Island Cabin/Decatur Island, WA

Citation for Future Work,
AIA Washington Chapter
Eastern Washington University,
Student Union Addition

Honor Award, AIA NW & Pacific Region
Marquand Retreat/Yakima, WA

1993
Honor Award, AIA Seattle Chapter
Marquand Retreat/Yakima, WA

Honor Award, AIA Seattle Chapter
Weaver/Bergh Residence/Bainbridge
Island, WA

Honor Award, AIA NW & Pacific Region
Boeing Cafeteria 9-12/Seattle, WA

Honor Award, AIA NW & Pacific Region
Jackson House/Decatur Island, WA

Merit Award, Drive-by Jury,
AIA NW & Pacific Region
Jackson House/Decatur Island, WA

Merit Award, Sunset Magazine
Roundy Residence/Coupeville, WA

Citation Award, Sunset Magazine
Marquand Retreat/Yakima, WA

Citation Award/Sunset Magazine
Noyes/Ryan Cabin/Decatur Island, WA

Award Winner,
Cedar Shake & Shingle Bureau
Lake Washington United Methodist
Church/Kirkland

Award Winner Metal in Architecture
The Boeing Cafeteria 9–12/Seattle, WA

Merit Award,
Masonry Institute of Washington
Adams Elementary School/Seattle, WA

1992
Honor Award, AIA NW & Pacific Region
Noyes/Ryan Cabin/Decatur Island, WA

Citation for Future Work,
AIA Seattle Chapter
Lakeside School Art Facility/Seattle, WA

Merit Award, ASLA
Meadowdale Beach Park/Lynnwood, WA

1991
Excellence in Planning & Design,
Record Houses Issue
Noyes/Ryan Cabin/Decatur Island, WA

Honor Award, AIA Seattle Chapter
Jackson House/Decatur Island, WA

Merit Award, AIA Seattle Chapter
Boeing Cafeteria 9–12/Seattle, WA

Citation for Future Work,
AIA Seattle Chapter
Poschman Residence/Orcas Island, WA

Design Award, American Wood Council
Noyes/Ryan Cabin/Decatur Island, WA

Honor Award, AIA NW & Pacific Region
Marine Technology Facility/Seattle, WA

Honor Award, AIA NW & Pacific Region
Noyes/Ryan Cabin/Decatur Island, WA

Daily Journal of Commerce/AIA Seattle
July Project of the Month
Univ. of Washington Fisheries Teaching &
Research Building

1990
Merit Award, AIA Seattle Chapter
Noyes/Ryan Cabin/Decatur Island, WA

Citation Award, AIA Seattle Chapter
Future Project,
Seattle Passenger Only Ferry Terminal

Merit Award, AIA Seattle Chapter
Future Project,
Charles Street Maintenance Facility
Seattle, WA

Merit Award, Sunset Magazine
Bolen Cabin/Decatur Island, WA

Merit Award, ASLA
Meadowdale Beach Park/Lynnwood, WA

Merit Award, AIA Seattle Chapter
Bolen Cabin/Decatur Island, WA

1989
Merit Award, Sunset Magazine
Bolen Cabin/Decatur Island, WA

Merit Award, ASLA
Meadowdale Beach Park/Lynnwood, WA

Merit Award, AIA Seattle Chapter
Evergreen State College/Art Studios
Addition

People's Choice Award, AIA Seattle Chapter
Bolen Cabin/Decatur Island, WA

1987
Honor Award, Sunset Magazine
Gorton/Bounds Cabin/Decatur Island, WA

Merit Award, Sunset Magazine
Metzger Residence/Lake Marcel, WA

High Honor Award,
National Lab of the Year Competition
Metro Environmental

Laboratories/Seattle, WA
Honor Award, AIA Seattle Chapter
Marine Technology Facility/Seattle, WA

1986
Honor Award AIA Seattle Chapter &
People's Choice Award
Metro Environmental
Laboratories/Seattle, WA

1985
Honor Award, American Wood Council
Aware Women's Shelter/Juneau, AL

Honor Award, AIA Seattle Chapter
& People's Choice Award
The Aware Women's Shelter/Juneau, AK

Honor Award, AIA Seattle Chapter
Gorton Bounds Cabin/Decatur Island, WA

People's Choice Award,
AIA Seattle Chapter
Gorton/Bounds Cabin/Decatur Island, WA

1983
Honor Award, Sunset Magazine
Mercy Residence/Lake Marcel, WA

Citation Award, American Wood Council
Cedar Hills Activities Building/Maple
Valley, WA

1982
Honor Award, AIA Seattle Chapter
Cedar Hills Activities Building/Maple
Valley, WA

Citation of Merit, National Plywood

Design Awards
Cedar Hills Activities Building/Maple
Valley, WA

Honor Award, AIA Seattle Chapter
Mercy Residence/Lake Marcel, WA

AIA Home of the Month
Mercy Residence/Lake Marcel, WA

1980
Finalist Award, The Fifth National
Passive Solar Competition
Kimmick Residence/Cle Elum, WA
Hansen Residence/Moses Lake, WA

227

BIOGRAPHIES OF THE PARTNERS

228

DAVID E. MILLER, FAIA

Architect and founding partner of the Miller/Hull Partnership. Born in Des Moines, Iowa in 1944, he received a Bachelor of Architecture in 1968 from Washington State University. The following two years were spent in the U.S. Peace Corps in Brasilia, Brazil, working on self-help housing. He attended the University of Illinois on a Plym Fellowship and received his Masters in Architecture in 1972. During this time Miller worked part time at the Chicago office of Skidmore Owings & Merrill.

After graduate studies Miller worked for architect Arthur Erikson of Vancouver, Canada, on the British Columbia Provincial Courthouse. In 1975 he joined Rhone & Iredale Architects where, in 1977, he was named partner and opened the RIA Seattle office with Robert Hull. In 1980 the Seattle office became independent from RIA and was renamed the Miller/Hull Partnership.

David Miller joined the University of Washington faculty in 1990 as an associate professor of architecture, teaching graduate design studio. He periodically directs the University of Washington's Architecture in Rome program, and has taught in Tokyo, Japan. In 1998 he received tenure and full professor status. Miller was named a Fellow by the American Institute of Architects in 1994.

ROBERT E. HULL, FAIA

Architect and founding partner of the Miller/Hull Partnership. Born in Moses Lake, Washington in 1945, he received a Bachelor of Architecture in 1968 from Washington State University in Pullman, twice receiving the Student Distinction award. Following graduation from 1968 to 1972 he served in the U.S. Peace Corps in Afghanistan, where he designed and built the headquarters for the National Tourism Agency and helped establish a school of architecture at Kabul University.

Upon returning to the states, he worked in the New York office of Marcel Breuer from 1972 to 1975. In 1975 Hull relocated to Vancouver, Canada to work in the offices of Rhone & Iredale Architects, where, in 1977 he was named partner and opened the RIA Seattle office with David Miller. In 1980 the Seattle office became independent from RIA and was renamed the Miller/Hull Partnership. In 1995 he was named a Fellow by the American Institute of Architects.

NORMAN H. STRONG, AIA

Architect and partner. Norman H. Strong was born in Moscow, Idaho in 1954, and received a cum laude Bachelor of Architecture degree in 1978 from Washington State University in Pullman, Washington. Strong joined Miller/Hull in 1979 and became a partner in 1985. Active in the American Institute of Architects, Strong was a board member for the Washington State AIA Council and the NW & Pacific Region, and served as Seattle Chapter president 1999–2000.

CRAIG A. CURTIS, AIA

Architect and partner of the Miller/Hull Partnership. Craig A. Curtis was born in Tonasket, Washington in 1960. He received a Bachelor of Architecture in 1983 and a Bachelor of Science in Construction Management in 1984 from Washington State University. After working at the Austin Hansen Fehlman Group in San Diego from 1984 to 1986 he joined Miller/Hull in 1987, becoming a partner in 1994.

CURRENT STAFF	Robert Hutchison	FORMER STAFF	Julie Kreigh	231
David Miller, Partner	Mike Jobes	Carla Allbee	Olivier Landa	
Robert Hull, Partner	Vanessa Kaneshiro	Chris Arthur	Amy Lelyveld	
Norman Strong, Partner	Chrys Kim	Deborah Battle	Rhonda Mauer	
Craig Curtis, Partner	Claudine Manio	Pete Bruner	Tom McCollum	
Steve Tatge, Sr. Associate	Michael Mariano	Dave Brunner	Andrew Michal	
Scott Wolf, Associate	Petra Michaely	Christopher Carlson	Tom Morris	
Sian Roberts, Associate	Doug Mikko	Victoria Carter	Christopher Osolin	
Stephen Southerland,	Katie Popolow	Philip Christofides	Christopher Patano	
Associate	Ron Rochon	Lene Copeland	Jana Rekosh	
Susan Kelly, Associate	Chad Rollins	Susan Cooper	Patrick Sheahan	
	Stacy Rowland	Susana Covarrubias	Cathi Scott	
Mark Adams	Grace Schlitt	Steve deKoch	Tracy Smith	
Ruth Baleiko	Teresa Shannon	Kathleen Dutcher	Aidan Stretch	
Kristin Bergman	Ted Shelton	Laurie Fanger	Daniel Mihaylo	
Renee Boone	Margaret Sprug	Allan Farkas	Mark Vanderzanden	
Allison Capen	Kurt Stolle	Laura Hafermann	Jennifer Wedderman	
Molly Cooper	Tricia Stuth	Gabriel Hadjiani	Peter Wolff	
Brian Court	Joyce Too	Annie Han	Holden Withington	
Amy DeDominicis	Eric Walter	John Hartung		
Huyen Huang	Richard Whealan	Lisa Kirkendall		

SELECTED BIBLIOGRAPHY

Books

Riera Ojeda,ed. *Ten Houses: Miller/Hull Partnership.* Gloucester, MA: Rockport Publishers, 1999.

Trulove, James Grayson and Il Kim, eds. *The New American Cottage–Innovations in Small-Scale Residential Architecture.* New York, NY: Whitney Library of Design, 1999. [Campbell Orchard Residence]

Zellner, Peter, ed. *Pacific Edge: Contemporary Architecture on the Pacific Rim.* New York: Rizzoli, 1998, 78–83. [Olympic College, Shelton, Washington, and Marquand Retreat]

Stuchin and Abramson, eds. *Waterside Homes.* Glen Cove NY: Rizzoli, 1998. [Novotny Cabin]

Galfetti, Gustau Gili, ed. *Casa Refugio (Private Retreats).* Barcelona, Spain: 1995. [Marquand Retreat]

Carmody and Sterling, eds. *Earth Sheltered Housing Design.* Minneapolis, MN: Van Nostrand Reinhold, 1985. [Mercy Residence]

Holthusen, Lance T., ed. *Earth Sheltering: The Form of Energy and the Energy of Form.* New York: Pergamon Press: 1981. [Kimmick Residence and Hansen Residence]

Articles

Olson, Sheri. "Feature Residence: Roddy Bale Residence" *Architectural Record* (July 2000): 204–209

Makovsky, Paul. "New Architecture Faces the Future." *Metropolis* (April 2000): 75. [Olympic College, Shelton]

Bertelsen, Ann, Peter O. Whiteley, and Daniel Gregory. "1999–2000 Western Home Awards–tower bridge." *Sunset Magazine* (October 1999): 126–127. [Michaels/Sisson Residence]

Olson, Sheri. "Yaquina Head gives visitors the key to a kingdom by the sea." *Architectural Record* (October 1999): 144–146.

Caldarelli, Mario. "Concavo, convesso–Olympic College Shelton" *L'Arca* (June 1999): 12–17.

"American Institute of Architects 1999 Honors and Awards" *Architectural Record* (May 1999): 136. [Olympic College, Shelton]

Thompson, William. "The Poetics of Stormwater." *Landscape Architecture* (January 1999): 58–63, 86 ff.

Cheek, Lawrence W. "A four-square house by Miller|Hull Partnership stands its ground beneath a dense wooded canopy." *Architecture Magazine* (December 1998): 84–89. [Michaels/Sisson Residence]

Boddy, Trevor. "Border Lines."
Architecture Magazine (May 1998):
140–143. Point Roberts Border Station]

Hinshaw, Mark. "Architecture
Waterworks. *Architecture Magazine*
(July 1997): 102–107.

Boddy, Trevor. "NW Federal Credit
Union, Seattle, Washington."
Architectural Record (June 1997):
140–143.

Thompson, William. "Mail-Order Pride."
Landscape Architecture (March 1997):
56–61.

Olson, Sheri. "A True Community
College." *Architectural Record*
(November, 1996): 90–93. [Olympic
College, Shelton]

"On the Boards" *Architecture Magazine*
(October 1996): 56. [Fremont Public
Association]

"Case Study: Patagonia Building a Model
for Green Planning." *Environmental
Building News* (September/October
1996): 8–9.

Albert, Fred. "Cabin fever." *Seattle
Magazine* (July 1996): 25. [Marquand
Retreat]

Canty, Donald. "Seattle Community
Centers Put Sustainability to the Test."
Places (Winter 1995): 78. [Garfield
Community Center]
"Vitality Wins the Day." *Progressive
Architecture* (December 1995): 35.
[Garfield Community Center; Olympic
College, Shelton]

"On the Boards." *Architecture Magazine*.
(July 1995): 39. [NW Federal Credit
Union]

Hinshaw, Mark. "New Public Outlook."
Architecture Magazine (June 1995):
78–83. [Garfield Community Center]

Biagi, Marco. "La valle dell' Eden" *Ville
Giardini* (Italy) (June 1995): 28–29.
[Marquand Retreat]

Henderson, Justin. "Retreat Into
Nature." *Architecture Magazine* (May
1994): 88. [Marquand Retreat]

"A bunker for weekend bunking." *Sunset
Magazine* (October 1993): 97–98.
[Marquand Retreat]

Henderson, Justin. "Structural Shade."
Architecture Magazine (October 1992):
72–75. [Boeing Cafeteria]

"Regional Portfolio–The Pacific
Northwest." *Architectural Record* (May
1990): 88–89. [Evergreen State College
Art Studios]

Hauser Magazine (November 1989):
150. [Gorton/Bounds Cabin]

Sachner, Paul M. "Maritime maneuvers."
Architectural Record (February 1989):
118–19. Seattle Central Community
College Marine Technology Center]

Murphy, Jim. "An Open Hideaway."
Progressive Architecture (December
1988): 96–97. [Gorton/Bounds Cabin]

"Award-winning cabins." *Sunset
Magazine* (September 1988): 71–72.
[Gorton/Bounds Cabin]

Home Magazine (July 1987):
[Gorton/Bounds Cabin]

"A Beautiful, Spare Long House."
Architecture Minnesota (May 1983).
[Cedar Hills Activities Building]

"Local Architects Honored With
Architecture + Energy Awards."
Northwest Environmental Review (Fall
1996). [NW Federal Credit Union]

PHOTO CREDITS

Page ii: Strode Eckert

Pages iv–v: James F. Housel

Page viii: James F. Housel

Page 2: Greg Krogstad

Pages 4–5: Miller/Hull

Page 7: James F. Housel

Page 8: Chris Eden

Page 10: Steven Cridland

Pages 13–14: James F. Housel

Page 15: Gary Ochsner

Page 16: Chris Eden

Page 19: Jim Fanning

Page 20: Art Grice

Page 21: Chris Eden

Pages 22 and 25: Strode Eckert

Page 29: James F. Housel

Pages 30–35: Chris Eden

Pages 37–38: Gary Ochsner

Page 40: Miller/Hull

Pages 43–47: Jim Fanning

Page 48: Miller/Hull

Pages 51–53: Michael Shopenn

Pages 54–59: Strode Eckert

Pages 60–65: Steven Cridland

Pages 66–71: James F. Housel

Pages 72 and 74: Chris Eden

Pages 76–77: Chris Eden

Page 79: Miller/Hull

Pages 80–85: Strode Eckert

Pages 86–90: Chris Eden

Page 95: Miller/Hull

Pages 98–121: James F. Housel

Pages 122–127: David Story

Pages 128–135: Strode Eckert

Pages136–141: James F. Housel

Pages 142–149: Strode Eckert

Page 151: Miller/Hull

Pages 152–155: James F. Housel

Page 156: Ernie Duncan

Pages 158–165: James F. Housel

Page 166: Art Grice

Page 168: James F. Housel

Pages 169–172: Art Grice

Pages 174–175: James F. Housel

Pages 176–178: Art Grice

Pages 179–186: James F. Housel

Page 187: Miller/Hull

Pages 188–190: Jay Dotson

Page 191: Miller/Hull

Page 192: Jay Dotson

Pages 194–199: James F. Housel

Pages 200–204: Steve Dubinsky

Pages 207–213: Art Grice

Page 215: Chris Eden

Page 220 (left): Miller/Hull
   (right): Gregory Minaker

Page 221: Michael Shopenn

Page 222: Miller/Hull

Page 223 (left): Chris Eden
   (right): Miller/Hull

Pages 229 and 231: James F. Housel